COLLINS GEM
CATS
a mine of information

COLLINS GEM
Chinese
ASTROLOGY

COLLINS GEM
Classic
BOOKS

COLLINS GEM
Classic
FILMS

COLLINS GEM
HORSES
& PONIES
a mine of information

INSECTS

COLLINS GEM
KINGS &
QUEENS
a mine of information

COLLINS GEM
MUSHROOMS
& TOADSTOOLS
a mine of information

COLLINS GEM
SNAKES
a mine of information

COLLINS GEM
SPIDERS
a mine of information

COLLINS GEM
STRESS
Survival Guide
a mine of information

COLLINS GEM
TAROT
a mine of information

COLLINS GEM
WINE
Guide
a mine of information

COLLINS GEM
WORLD
atlas
a mine of information

COLLINS GEM
YOGA
a mine of information

COLLINS GEM
ZODIAC
Types
a mine of information

D0774853

COLLINS GEM

FENG SHUI

Richard Craze

HarperCollins*Publishers*

Richard Craze has practised as a feng shui consultant and has worked closely with Chinese communities both in London and Bristol. He has studied Taoism extensively and has taught meditation, yoga and stress management in the UK and overseas. He is currently a full-time freelance writer.

The Printer's Devil would like to thank Apple Computers, *Feng Shui for Modern Living*, and Natural Harmony of Plymouth for their kind assistance in supplying images and artifacts for use in this book. Thanks are also due to David Braysher for drawing the illustrations on pp. 17, 24, 27 and 32.

HarperCollins Publishers
PO Box, Glasgow G4 0NB

First published 1999

Reprint 10 9 8 7 6 5 4 3 2 1 0

ISBN 0 00 472316 3

Printed in Italy by Amadeus S.p.A.

Contents

Introduction

Few people here in the West would have predicted the phenomenal interest that has developed in feng shui in recent years. At first it may seem surprising that such an art, such a skill that is rooted so deeply in Chinese culture, history and philosophy should have proven so popular outside of China or Hong Kong, but that it is so is testimony to its continuing relevance to modern lifestyles across many different cultures. The *Collins Gem Feng Shui* aims to provide a simple and accessible explanation of what feng shui is, how it works, what it can do for you and, most importantly, how you can do it yourself.

Feng shui has been practised in China for several thousand years and during that time it has come under the influence of Buddhism, Confucianism, Taoist priests and scholars of many differing philosophies and, quite naturally, it has been subject to changes and additions. Some of these have little relevance in the modern world while others are still valid and important. What I have tried to do in this book is to cut away some of the older, more superstitious aspects of feng shui and present a version that is both valid and practical, workable and understandable.

I have tried to adhere to a simple rule while writing this book: does it work and can it be seen to work? In practice what this has meant is that if I don't under-stand some aspect of feng shui practice or use it then I have not included it. For this reason, the feng shui presented in this book is what I would regard as a more pure form. It goes back to the very fundamentals of feng shui and prunes away some of the later additions. For example, you will see that I have used the Former Heaven Sequence throughout, in contrast to the modern habit of adopting the Later Heaven Sequence. I have also used the traditional way that the Chinese orientate their maps and compasses with south at the top. In Chinese society, south is the most important direction so it makes sense to maintain this in a subject which relies so heavily on compass direction. For Western readers, this can be initially confusing but it does give a more oriental and exotic feel to feng shui which makes it feel somehow right; as you work through this book, I hope you agree.

Feng shui has different forms, different schools of thought and has experienced many twists and turns throughout its long history. However, a common thread running through all aspects of feng shui of whatever persuasion is the emphasis on people taking responsibility for their lives. No one can say what is right or wrong for you so when you practise feng shui, follow your heart. If it feels right for you, then do it; if it doesn't, then don't. And don't forget – have fun!

Richard Craze
Devon, 1999

THE PRINCIPLES OF FENG SHUI

Feng shui (pronounced *feng shoy*) is partly a skill, partly an art form and partly an intuitive approach to how we live. It is very ancient and comes originally from China where it has been in use for at least three thousand years. Put quite simply, feng shui is a method of arranging our environment to be as beneficial as possible to us. It requires a certain knowledge of how, according to Chinese Taoist thought, cosmic energy – known as *ch'i* (pronounced *chee, see p.15*) – moves around us all the time. Once we know how this energy moves, we can arrange our homes, our furniture, and even ourselves, to make best use of it. In fact, once we know how to manipulate the ch'i, we can even use that information to improve our health as ch'i is capable of stagnating or even being in itself unhealthy.

feng = wind

shui = water

So seriously is the subject taken in Hong Kong, that the feng shui practitioner is as important to a new building project as the architect.

Feng shui is thus the knowledge of how ch'i can be used to best effect in each of our lives. If the ch'i around us is bad or unpleasant – when it is known as *sha* which means 'noxious vapour' – we will suffer from bad luck (which according to feng shui practitioners isn't 'luck' or the action of fate at all but the influence of sha), stagnating relationships, poor health, lack of motivation and general all-round lethargy and sluggishness. Yet once we have improved the flow of ch'i around us, our health picks up, as do our relationships, luck, money-earning potential and happiness.

Feng shui translated means 'wind and water' which is how ch'i is seen to flow. And, like both wind and water, it is subject to being blocked, impeded, diverted, speeded up, slowed down, corrupted and improved. You only have to think about how a river can go from being a sluggish back water to a raging torrent to get the idea. You can dam water to slow it down or clear any obstacles to speed it up. Ch'i is the same. The skill in feng shui is knowing how to speed it up – but not too much so that it is overpowering – or to slow it down – again not too much so that it becomes stagnant.

How Feng Shui Works

DIFFERENT SCHOOLS

Over the centuries, various ways of practising feng shui have emerged. There are three main schools, each being quite different in its approach. The edges of these three schools of feng shui have become blurred and they overlap in many places but they can be summed up as:

1 **Compass or Lo P'an Feng Shui**. This relies heavily on the use of a traditional feng shui compass, called a *lo p'an*, which can have up to 64 concentric rings containing information which a feng shui consultant would use to determine whether your house was right for you. Compass feng shui is very traditional

The lo p'an or feng shui compass

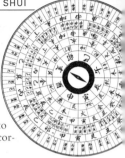

in China as a service provided for burial. The Chinese are very superstitious and believe that a person buried in a 'wrong' place will return to haunt the living – a 'hungry ghost' – and that it is essential to make sure the grave is aligned correctly.

2 **Directional or Pa kwa Feng Shui**. This is feng shui that uses the direction your house faces to arrive at information as well as dividing your house up into eight areas or enrichments – the *pa kwa* (sometimes spelt bagua) – that govern every area of your life such as relationships, family, career and health.

3 **Intuitive or Yin Yang Feng Shui**. This branch of feng shui is more concerned with the way energy flows in and around your home and how you fit in with that energy. It would seek to find a balance between yin and yang (*see p. 12*) and would be termed 'form' feng shui – the shape and structure of your home as well as its furnishings.

We will cover all three schools of thought in the course of this book but as we don't all have access to a traditional feng shui compass, the first will be dealt with only generally. Directional feng shui is very formal and can become confusing if your home doesn't fit exactly into a pa kwa shape but it is a useful way for beginners to learn feng shui. Yin Yang feng shui, which is the one we will work with mainly, is instinctive and intuitive and allows you a greater input and control. But our edges will be blurred and we will use all three in different ways.

Chinese Spelling

For many years in the West we used a system of Chinese spelling known as the Wade Giles system; this gave us such names as Peking. There is now however a newer system in use called 'pinyin' which gives us 'Beijing' instead of 'Peking'. It also makes *ch'i* become *qi*. Whilst I am happy with Beijing, I cannot find it in my heart to use qi and so I have used ch'i throughout this book. It also explains why there may be differences in spelling of such things as *pa kua* (*bagua*). And the oldest classic of all – the *I Ching* – becomes the *Yi Jing*. Fortunately, *feng shui* is the same under both spelling systems.

Feng Shui and Taoism

For a proper understanding of feng shui, an appreciation of the Chinese – specifically the Taoist – view of the universe is a key element. Taoism is the original religion of China although it could be considered more of a philosophy as it lacks any deity which might qualify it as a religion. Taoists believe that originally there was the empty cosmos. Into that cosmos came energy – ch'i – and from that energy matter was made. From the matter, the Earth and all in it was brought into being.

YIN AND YANG

Taoists also believe that everything in the universe is shaped by two cosmic forces, known as *Yin* (negative energy) and *Yang* (positive energy). These forces are in constant opposition but when combined, they constitute a balanced whole, a perfect harmony of the *Tao* or The Way. According to the Taoists, everything can be regarded as containing various degrees of Yin or Yang – but there is always a flow between the two, always a small part of something which is the other and ready to grow or transform into its opposite. This is why, in a yin/yang symbol there is always a tiny dot of the opposite in each part.

The dots represent the belief that everything contains the seed of its opposite within it

Taoists believe that these two opposite forces are what generates the ch'i and that ch'i is constantly flowing between yin and yang. There has to be a balance between them and ch'i is seeking that balance constantly. Where balance is achieved, good fortune will flow. If one or other force dominates then an imbalance will be created and problems will inevitably result.

CHARACTERISTICS OF YIN AND YANG

While Yin and Yang are generally seen in terms of being negative and positive forces, they are also seen to represent specific aspects of the world around us and of the human condition. These attributes are shown in the table overleaf.

Although Yin and Yang are seen as opposites, they are not in discord, nor should they be seen as in opposition as in the Western idea of good and evil constantly struggling for supremacy over each other. Instead, they should be seen as complimentary, with energy flowing naturally and gracefully from one state to the next – from yin to yang and from yang to yin. It's a bit like life itself: we are born, which Taoists would consider a yin state; we live – a yang state – and we die – back to yin again. The sun rises and a new day begins – a yang state – and when the day is done, it gets dark and it is night-time – a yin state. There is no opposition in any of this. You cannot have one without the other and so it is with yin and yang. Neither can exist without the other to help it and it is ch'i that binds the two forces together and permits the transformation of one to the other.

YIN	YANG
inner	outer
down	up
north	south
matter	spirit
creation	heaven
earth	sky
negative	positive
passive	active
female	male
receptive	creative
dark	light
night	day
cold	heat
soft	hard
wet	dry
winter	summer
shadow	sunshine

The various aspects of the universe and the human condition represented by the negative Yin and the positive Yang energies

Ch'i

Ch'i is energy – cosmic energy. It can be likened to the Hindu prana or the Christian Holy Spirit. You can see it as vital life force. You imagine it as a source of light and energy, invisible charged particles of power.

When ch'i flows well there is harmony and balance, and when it stagnates, it is believed to be the cause of many, if not all, illnesses. It can be seen as the main principle underpinning the Tao. Ch'i is the unseen life force that flows through and around everything, animating it. We cannot see, touch, taste, hear or feel ch'i but we are aware of it by its effect: creation is ch'i taking shape, while at death, living ch'i departs.

Manipulating the way ch'i flows in and around our dwellings is the art of feng shui. Feng shui can be seen as aligning our dwellings and ourselves to receive the maximum benefit of life-giving ch'i.

TYPES OF CH'I

There are four main types of ch'i which are shown in the table overleaf. From this, you can see the connection established between ch'i, yin and yang, and the compass directions.

CH'I AND YOUR HOME

As you open a door, you allow ch'i to enter into your home. Ch'i brings vitality and life into your house. It

TYPES OF CH'I

- **Sheng ch'i** – wise ch'i from the east
- **Yang ch'i** – invigorating ch'i from the south
- **T'sang ch'i** – nurturing ch'i from the north
- **Sha ch'i** – disruptive ch'i from the west

also picks up residue energy from where it has passed. For example, if your house faces an undertakers, it will pick up grief or if it faces a prison, it will pick up pain. However, if your house faces a beautiful landscape of fields and woods and streams then that is what the ch'i will bring with it. But don't despair – if your house faces something unpleasant there are remedies you can use to purify or correct the ch'i as it enters your home. We will look at these remedies later on (see p.35).

CH'I AND THE COMPASS

As well as picking up residue energy, ch'i also changes its quality depending on which direction it is flowing from. Each of the four main compass directions has its own quality which traditionally has always been associated with one of the four celestial animals of Chinese mythology.

1 From the south the ch'i is invigorating and lucky. This is the area of the Red Phoenix – the bird of the summer and good fortune.

2 From the north comes nurturing ch'i, from the area of the Black Tortoise. This ch'i is sleepy and mysterious which matches the Black Tortoise – the animal of the winter. This type of ch'i is also sometimes represented as a snake.

3 The west is home to the White Tiger. This ch'i is unpredictable and can be disruptive.

4 The east is home to the Gold (sometimes known as the Green) Dragon – a protective, kind ch'i which brings wisdom and culture.

From these four animals you can also see why the Chinese use the four colours of red, black, white and gold so often. Ideally you'd have low flat hills to the west so the power of the white tiger is lessened, while you would want good sloping dragon hills to the east to have as much wise ch'i as possible flowing down towards the house. To the south there should be a flat open view, preferably with a meandering stream, to encourage all that invigorating ch'i. And to the north there can be more hills – even mountains – to protect and nurture.

The Five Elements

The theory of the Five Aspects or Elements (*Wu Hsing*) s central to much of Oriental wisdom, medicine and philosophy. The Five Elements are

Earth   Wood   Fire   Metal   Water

The Chinese believe that these elements influence our daily lives and our environment through constant interaction in a series of cyclical relationships in which some elements help others and some, unfortunately, hinder others. The table opposite show how each element relates to the others.

ELEMENTAL HELPS AND HINDRANCES

- **Earth**: helps metal, is helped by fire but hinders water and is hindered by wood

- **Fire**: helps earth, is helped by wood but hinders metal and is hindered by water

- **Water**: helps wood, is helped by metal but hinders fire and is hindered by earth

- **Metal**: helps water, is helped by earth but hinders wood and is hindered by fire

- **Wood**: helps fire, is helped by water but hinders earth and is hindered by metal

You might like to see it as a sort of collection of tools or parts of nature. For instance wood helps fire – fire quite literally can't burn without the wood to fuel it. And wood needs the water to help it grow. But wood is also hindered by metal – an axe cuts wood pretty well. And wood, in turn, hinders earth – its roots (if you see wood as a tree) break up the earth.

Likewise, water helps wood by providing nourishment and is helped by metal – a metal bucket carries water extremely well. But water hinders fire – nothing better for putting fire out and is hindered by earth because the earth turns the water into mud.

THE FIVE ELEMENTS AND PERSONALITY

The five elements can also be viewed as representing different aspects of our personality or character. The Theory of the Five Aspects or Elements suggests that, whilst we are a combination of all of the elements, the characteristics of one particular element tends to predominate over the others in our personality.

1. Earth – *T'u* – The Diplomat: a moderate person with a great sense of loyalty who likes to pay attention to detail but can be stubborn. They like to be needed and seek harmony and balance in their lives. They should avoid damp places.

2. Fire – *Huo* – The Magician: a compassionate person who likes pleasure and excitement. They enjoy being in love and hate being bored. They are very communicative and intuitive. They should avoid hot places.

3. Water – *Shui* – The Philosopher: an imaginative, honest person who is clever, knowledgeable and independent. They can be a bit secretive but they are tough and resourceful. They should avoid cold places.

4. Metal – *Chin* – The Catalyst: they are organised and like to be in control. They have a need to be right and to have order and cleanliness around them. They appreciate quality in their lives and should avoid places that are too dry.

5. Wood – *Mu* – The Pioneer: wood people are expansive and purposeful. They are practical and like to be busy. They can be very competitive. They should avoid windy places.

It can be helpful when applying feng shui to your own environment, to know which element type you are, not least because each needs a different type of house, facing a different direction, a different location and a different environment in order to maximise the flow of ch'i. These needs can present problems if you have to share your home with others who are probably different elemental types.

OTHER ASSOCIATIONS OF THE FIVE ELEMENTS

Each of these five elements also rule or influence parts of the body, emotional expressions, colours, tastes and energies, as shown in the table overleaf.

IDENTIFYING YOUR ELEMENT

By now you are probably wondering which element you are. According to Chinese philosophy it all depends on the year you were born and particularly the last digit of that year. If you were born in a year ending in

- 0 – you are yang metal

- 1 – you are yin metal

- 2 – you are yang water

- 3 – you are yin water

ASSOCIATIONS OF THE FIVE ELEMENTS

	Wood	Fire	Earth	Metal	Water
Face	Eyes	Tongue	Mouth	Nose	Ears
Body	Tendons	Pulse	Muscle	Skin/hair	Bones
Expression	Anger	Gaiety	Thought	Worry	Fright
Colour	Green	Red	Yellow	White	Black
Taste	Sour	Bitter	Sweet	Pungent	Salt
Energy	Wind	Hot	Wet	Dry	Cold
Season	Spring	Summer	Late summer	Autumn	Winter
Direction	East	South	Centre	West	North

- 4 – you are yang wood
- 5 – you are yin wood
- 6 – you are yang fire
- 7 – you are yin fire
- 8 – you are yang earth
- 9 – you are yin earth

You can see there are two types of each element – the

yang and the yin. Yang types will be more extrovert and energetic while yin types will be more introvert and quieter.

Obviously, whether you are a yin or yang type of element will affect you. Yang types like darker, cooler houses while yin types tend to prefer lighter, more spacious accommodation. This is because we are always seeking the balance and harmony of the other energy force: because yang is light it seeks the dark, and because yin is dark it seeks the light. It is the same with the elements.

• **Fire**, associated with the south, the Red Phoenix (*see p.17*) seeks the cool of the north.

• **Water**, associated with the north, the Black Tortoise, seeks the heat of the south.

• **Wood**, associated with the east, the Gold Dragon, seeks the unpredictability of the west.

• **Metal**, associated with the west, the White Tiger, seeks the wisdom and calmness of the east.

• **Earth** occupies the centre and is comfortable with most directions but always seeks to be the centre of things.

From this you can see why two people sharing the same home may well prefer two very differing decorating styles. Knowing which element you are can therefore be helpful in striking a balance.

THE FIVE ELEMENTS AND THE COMPASS

So, these elements form five parts of a compass – with earth being the centre, fire the south, water the north, wood the east and metal the west. If you were to lay this out into a square you get the beginnings of the *Lo Shu* magic square which is extremely important in feng shui.

The Lo Shu Square

The origins of the Lo Shu square are to be found in an ancient Chinese legend. Some 4,000 years ago, a giant turtle surfaced from the River Lo in central China and

on its shell were nine clusters of circular markings. Each cluster comprised between one and nine dots which were arranged in a three-by-three grid pattern. The nine numbers were so arranged that if you added together any three, whether vertically, horizontally or diagonally on the grid, the total is always fifteen – magic indeed!

The pattern of dots on the turtle's shell from which the Lo Shu derived

Because numbers were of great significance in Chinese culture, the arrangement of

the Lo Shu rapidly assumed a symbolic importance
and associations were made which linked other aspects
of Taoist belief to the Lo Shu square.

LO SHU ASSOCIATIONS

From the table of associations for the Five Elements
(*see p.22*), we can add a range of detail to each box on
Lo Shu square once we have positioned each of the
Five Elements themselves. In the centre we position
earth and in the top centre square, fire. Water goes in
the bottom centre and wood in the left centre. This
leaves metal which goes in the middle right. This gives
the following arrangement:

We can then add additional information such as compass directions and seasons. This now gives

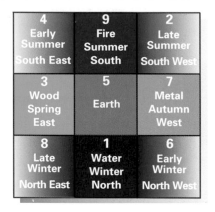

4 Early Summer South East	9 Fire Summer South	2 Late Summer South West
3 Wood Spring East	5 Earth	7 Metal Autumn West
8 Late Winter North East	1 Water Winter North	6 Early Winter North West

Note that unlike Western compasses, south is at the top instead of north, which is the traditional Chinese placing.

If we were to now draw diagonal lines across the four outer corners of the lo shu square, we get the traditional octagonal shape which is very important to feng shui: the *pa kwa*.

The Pa Kwa and the Eight Trigrams

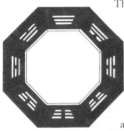

The pa kwa octagon, used in conjunction with eight special symbols (known as *trigrams*), is a common diagnostic tool in the Compass school of feng shui and is used to determine which area of a plot, house or room is in need of attention to improve the flow of ch'i.

THE EIGHT TRIGRAMS

Ignoring the centre area of the pa kwa for the moment, each of the other eight segments (or sides) is allocated a symbol known as a trigram. In fact, in Chinese, *pa* means eight and *kwa* means trigrams. Trigrams comprise different combinations of three solid and broken lines; the *yang line* is solid (—) while the *yin line* is broken (– –).

As with each square of the lo shu, each trigram has various associations. The eight trigrams are listed below along with their Chinese names, its English translation, and the seasons and compass points they are each associated with.

THE EIGHT TRIGRAMS

- **Ch'ien**: The Creative
  summer • south • fire • 9

- **Tui**: The Lake
  early summer • south east • 4

- **Li**: The Clinging
  spring • east • wood • 3

- **Chen**: The Thunder
  late winter • north east • 8

- **K'un**: The Receptive
  winter • north • water • 1

- **Ken**: The Mountain
  early winter • north west • 6

- **K'an**: The Dangerous
  autumn • west • metal • 7

- **H'sun**: The Wind
  late summer • south west • 2

HEAVEN SEQUENCES

The eight trigrams are said to have been created by Fu Hsi, a legendary emperor of China sometime around 3000 BC. Around 1100 BC, another emperor, Wen, further expanded them to make the 64 hexagrams (six-line symbols) of the *I Ching* (*The Book of Changes*), part oracle, part book of magic, part philosophical guide. One of the most sacred texts in China, it is also one of the most remarkable works of literature from any culture.

Emperor Wen also rearranged the order of the trigrams with regard to which compass direction each was assigned to on the pa kwa. The original order is called the *Former Heaven Sequence* and the later arrangement the *Later Heaven Sequence*. Because the feng shui remedies to be actioned differ under each sequence because of the differing placement of the trigrams, this divides most feng shui practitioners up into two schools: those who use the Former Heaven Sequence and those who use the Later Heaven Sequence.

The Former Heaven Sequence of trigrams was originally evolved for use in feng shui. It is a logical and rational way of laying out the compass directions with yin and yang opposite each other at the north and south, as well as polarities opposite each other and wind opposite thunder, mountain opposite lake, water opposite fire and heaven opposite earth – it all makes sense and fits together perfectly. The Later Heaven Sequence was evolved for use with the *I Ching*. Whilst the two do go hand-in-hand in many respects, the sequences do not. The Later Heaven Sequence seems to throw up a lot of anomalies for feng shui purposes. For instance, in the former sequence the children enrichment is put in the north east where it is protected by the north nurturing ch'i and the east ch'i of wisdom. In the later sequence children is put in the west – subject to unpredictable and potentially dangerous ch'i. Throughout this book, the former sequence is used with reference to the trigrams and the correspondences which follow from them.

The Later Heaven Sequence was modified by Emperor Wen around 1,000 BC and it has never been satisfactorily explained as to why the new order was suggested.

The Eight Enrichments

As we've said, the pa kwa is commonly used as a diagnostic tool to identify which area of your house, office or any other location is in need of attention to improve the flow of ch'i through it and in doing so, improve certain aspects of your life. The pa kwa does this by linking specific areas of influence common to everyone's life (known as the Eight Enrichments or Aspirations) with compass directions and hence with each of the eight trigrams. The areas of enrichments are shown opposite.

THE EIGHT ENRICHMENTS

- Fame and ambition
- Wealth and acquisitions
- Wisdom and learning
- Children and family
- Relationships
- Friendships
- Pleasures
- Health and happiness

THE ENRICHMENTS AND THE TRIGRAMS

Each of the these enrichments is associated with one of
the trigrams. However, as we've already discussed (*see
p.29*), depending on which heaven sequence you are
following, the position of each trigram on the pa kwa
will vary and with it, the enrichment assigned to it.
The two systems are compared below.

FORMER SEQUENCE

LATER SEQUENCE

Fame	south	*Fame*
Wealth	south east	*Wealth*

FORMER SEQUENCE   **LATER SEQUENCE**

Wisdom	☰	**east**	*Family/Health*
Children	☳	**north east**	*Education*
Relationships	☵	**north**	*Career*
Friends	☱	**north west**	*Friends*
Pleasure	☴	**west**	*Children*
Health	☷	**south west**	*Relationships*

Transferring the Former Heaven Sequence enrichments to the pa kwa gives the following:

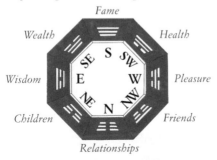

Fame

Wealth   *Health*

Wisdom   *Pleasure*

Children   *Friends*

Relationships

Ideally, our front door would open to the south and enable us to benefit from invigorating ch'i (*see p.16*) for ch'i types) as we step out into our fame area. If this were so, the back of our house would face north where we would expect to find our relationships, friends and children – all benefiting from nurturing and warm ch'i rolling down from the protective black hills of the tortoise. We would have our pleasure area in the west where it might have a little colour added to it by the unpredictable ch'i of the white tiger. And our wisdom would be in the east, ready to benefit from the accumulated wisdom of the dragon.

However, life is rarely that simple and often our front door opens into another compass direction. This is where you have to do a little work. You'll need a compass to work out where your front door faces if you don't already know. Now, suppose it faces south west. This would mean you were opening your front door into your health area.

Work out which direction your front door faces. Draw a pa kwa shape on some paper and mark on it the Former Heaven Sequence enrichments around the outside, as on page 34. Check which area your fame is opening into. We now need to check what happens to all the other areas when you shift the pa kwa round so that the fame area is positioned in the same direction as your front door faces. With fame in this position, write the names of the eight enrichments inside the octagon in order as shown overleaf.

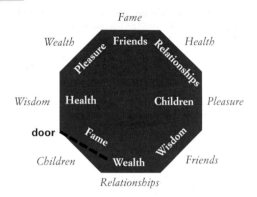

This example is for someone with a front door facing
north east which puts their fame area (internal) into
their children area (external). Now you have to do
some work and think about how that could affect them.
Is this the house of someone who is very good with
children? Perhaps makes their reputation by looking
after children? A nursery worker or a child care
officer? Then consider what facing north east does to
the rest of the enrichments. We can quickly go round
each one and see what possible effects this may have.

1 Wealth in Relationships – have they married into
  money? Are they looking to their partner to support
  them?

2 Wisdom in Friendships – are they a wise counsellor to their friends? Do their friends seek them out for advice?

3 Children in Pleasure – does this tie in with their fame in children? Do they find great pleasure in looking after or dealing with children?

4 Relationships in Health – are they buoyed up by being in a good relationship? When their relationships goes wrong, do they suffer from ill health?

5 Friends in Fame – do they have lots of friends? Are they gregarious and popular?

6 Pleasure in Wealth – do they enjoy spending money? Are they shopaholics?

7 Health in Wisdom – do they study health matters? Are they great readers of health books?

And back to fame in children.

You can do this for you own house. Check the direction that your front door faces and how it affects all eight enrichments.

The Eight Remedies

Having checked your own home in this way and considered what may be wrong with any particular area of your life, you can then decide how best to tackle the problem. If you feel that there is nothing amiss with any particular enrichment in your life, then there is no need to change anything. If, however, you feel things could be improved then you can add certain 'remedies' to an enrichment area. This can change the flow of ch'i and so remove or reduce any problems in a particular area of your life. There are eight remedies and each has its own 'best' enrichment that it works in. However, you may find that certain remedies work better in some areas than others and you may have to experiment in order to get the best results.

THE EIGHT REMEDIES

1 Light: e.g. lights, mirrors

2 Sound: e.g. chimes, bells, water

3 Colour: use strong bright colours

4 Life: e.g. plants, fish, pets

5 Movement: e.g. wind chimes, mobiles

6 Stillness: e.g. statues, rocks (in gardens)

7 Mechanical/electrical: keep in the appropriate room

8 Straight Lines: e.g. scrolls, bamboo flutes

LIGHT

This remedy includes not only room lights, but also mirrors and any reflective surfaces. Of these, mirrors are perhaps the mostly commonly used feng shui remedy and they can be incorporated into almost any environment. Mirrors will:

• reflect bad ch'i back out of a building

• encourage good ch'i in by drawing in an attractive outside view

• lighten and enlarge small dark rooms

• deflect ch'i around hidden corners

Lights should be as bright as possible without causing glare and when they are supplemented by mirrors, both can completely transform a room.

Unlike in the West, the Chinese make great use of lights outside of their property and also in their gardens to fill in areas where ch'i is absent or stagnating.

Wind chimes

SOUND

Anything that makes sound, melodic preferably, can be used as a remedy: bells, metal mobiles, bamboo tubes, etc. Wind chimes in particular are seen as a common feature of Chinese interior design, often without it being realised that they are an important feng shui remedy. This remedy works by disturbing stagnant ch'i through the swirls and eddies of sound in the air. Wind chimes also act as gentle alarms to alert us to comings and goings in our house. Harmonious sounds also attract lucky ch'i and are said to encourage wealth into buildings. The sound of water flowing is particularly auspicious and fountains can be seen both as movement and sound remedies.

COLOUR

According to Chinese tradition, colour – particularly red and black – can be used to stimulate the flow of ch'i,. Red and black are lucky colours associated with attracting wealth. Subdued colour schemes are more common in the West but a sudden patch of bright strong colour in a stagnating room can stimulate ch'i quite effectively.

LIFE

For this remedy, any living object –
plant or animals – can be used. Plants
are mainly used to fill in areas without ch'i and also to hide disruptive
sharp corners that jut into rooms.
Large plants can be used to slow ch'i
down when it would otherwise move
too swiftly along straight lines. Fish in
aquariums also serve the same purpose. Because in Chinese, 'fish' and
'money' use the same word, fish
become living symbols of wealth.
This is why aquariums are often close
to the cash register in Chinese restau-
rants – it encourages you to spend
freely.

Burning incense

MOVEMENT

Any moving object – flags,
silk banners, ribbons, fountains, wind chimes, mobiles
and weather vanes – can be
used wherever ch'i needs to
be stimulated or deflected.
These should be made of
natural materials and use
the natural power of the
wind wherever possible.
The smoke from incense can

also be considered as movement and so be used as a remedy. Flowing water brings positive ch'i to a building providing it moves gently and gurgles, rather than quickly and roars.

STILLNESS

Where ch'i is flowing too fast, a statue, large rock or other substantial inanimate object can prove effective in slowing it down. This is particularly true in gardens where the path to a front gate can cause the ch'i to leave too quickly. Statues should blend into their environment.

MECHANICAL/ELECTRICAL

Traditionally, this remedy usually meant machinery but nowadays it can be extended to include any electrical equipment in our daily lives: televisions, hi-fis, electrical

fans, and, increasingly, computers. Electrical equipment stimulates ch'i but sometimes can overdo it so it is advisable to minimise the number of appliances we use around the home or office. Electricity and ch'i both need to be treated with respect.

STRAIGHT LINES

The Chinese use flutes, swords, scrolls, bamboo tubes, and fans to break up ch'i when it moves heavily or sluggishly, especially along beams and down long corridors.

WHICH REMEDY TO USE WHERE?

How and when you would use these eight remedies will be explained in the next section. For the moment, however, it is worth knowing in which of the eight enrichments each works best:

- **Light** remedies are traditionally associated with your *fame enrichment*

- **Sound** remedies are associated with your *friends enrichment*

- **Colour** remedies are associated with your *children enrichment*

- **Life** remedies are associated with your *wealth enrichment*

- **Movement** remedies are associated with your *relationship enrichment*

- **Stillness** remedies are associated with your *pleasure enrichment*

- **Mechanical object** remedies are associated with your *wisdom enrichment*

- **Straight line** remedies are associated with your *health enrichment*

The Chinese Calendar

In previous sections we looked at how the four compass directions each has its own type of ch'i – and its own element. Another factor that comes into play is the Chinese system of what might be termed 'astrology'. It isn't really astrology as the term is commonly used as it doesn't aim or attempt to predict anything; instead it merely classifies people according to when they were born. It is also unlike Western astrology in the sense that it doesn't need to know 'where' you were born, only when. Chinese astrology needs to know the year, the month and the hour of your birth. Each of these three times has one of twelve animals ascribed to it:

Rat   Ox   Tiger   Hare

Dragon   Horse   Goat

Snake

Cockerel   Monkey   Dog   Pig

Each of these animals has particular qualities and characteristics. According to the year of your birth you are a certain type of animal. These animals are repeated five times every twelve years to make a sixty-year cycle. Each of the animals gets five different types according to the year and each is a different element. You need to know when you where born and check this with the table following. Once you know your animal you can work out which direction is best for you to face in – or rather your house to face in.

1900	31 Jan 1900	18 Feb 1901	Yang	Metal	Rat
1901	19 Feb 1901	7 Feb 1902	Yin	Metal	Ox
1902	8 Feb 1902	28 Jan 1903	Yang	Water	Tiger
1903	29 Jan 1903	15 Feb 1904	Yin	Water	Hare
1904	6 Feb 1904	3 Feb 1905	Yang	Wood	Dragon
1905	4 Feb 1905	24 Jan 1906	Yin	Wood	Snake
1906	25 Jan 1906	12 Feb 1907	Yang	Fire	Horse
1907	13 Feb 1907	1 Feb 1908	Yin	Fire	Goat
1908	2 Feb 1908	21 Jan 1909	Yang	Earth	Monkey
1909	22 Jan 1909	9 Feb 1910	Yin	Earth	Cockerel
1910	10 Feb 1910	29 Jan 1911	Yang	Metal	Dog
1911	30 Jan 1911	17 Feb 1912	Yin	Metal	Pig

1912	18 Feb 1912	5 Feb 1913	Yang	Water	Rat
1913	6 Feb 1913	25 Jan 1914	Yin	Water	Ox
1914	26 Jan 1914	13 Feb 1915	Yang	Wood	Tiger
1915	14 Feb 1915	2 Feb 1916	Yin	Wood	Hare
1916	3 Feb 1916	22 Jan 1917	Yang	Fire	Dragon
1917	23 Jan 1917	10 Feb 1918	Yin	Fire	Snake
1918	11 Feb 1918	31 Jan 1919	Yang	Earth	Horse
1919	1 Feb 1919	19 Feb 1920	Yin	Earth	Goat
1920	20 Feb 1920	7 Feb 1921	Yang	Metal	Monkey
1921	8 Feb 1921	27 Jan 1922	Yin	Metal	Cockerel
1922	28 Jan 1922	15 Feb 1923	Yang	Water	Dog
1923	16 Feb 1923	4 Feb 1924	Yin	Water	Pig
1924	5 Feb 1924	24 Jan 1925	Yang	Wood	Rat
1925	25 Jan 1925	12 Feb 1926	Yin	Wood	Ox
1926	13 Feb 1926	1 Feb 1927	Yang	Fire	Tiger
1927	2 Feb 1927	22 Jan 1928	Yin	Fire	Hare
1928	23 Jan 1928	9 Feb 1929	Yang	Earth	Dragon
1929	10 Feb 1929	29 Jan 1930	Yin	Earth	Snake
1930	30 Jan 1930	16 Feb 1931	Yang	Metal	Horse

1931	17 Feb 1931	5 Feb 1932	Yin	Metal	Goat
1932	6 Feb 1932	25 Jan 1933	Yang	Water	Monkey
1933	26 Jan 1933	13 Feb 1934	Yin	Water	Cockerel
1934	14 Feb 1934	3 Feb 1935	Yang	Wood	Dog
1935	4 Feb 1935	23 Jan 1936	Yin	Wood	Pig
1936	24 Jan 1936	10 Feb 1937	Yang	Fire	Rat
1937	11 Feb 1937	30 Jan 1938	Yin	Fire	Ox
1938	31 Jan 1938	18 Feb 1939	Yang	Earth	Tiger
1939	19 Feb 1939	7 Feb 1940	Yin	Earth	Hare
1940	8 Feb 1940	26 Jan 1941	Yang	Metal	Dragon
1941	27 Jan 1941	14 Feb 1942	Yin	Metal	Snake
1942	15 Feb 1942	4 Feb 1943	Yang	Water	Horse
1943	5 Feb 1943	24 Jan 1944	Yin	Water	Goat
1944	25 Jan 1944	12 Feb 1945	Yang	Wood	Monkey
1945	13 Feb 1945	1 Feb 1946	Yin	Wood	Cockerel
1946	2 Feb 1946	21 Jan 1947	Yang	Fire	Dog
1947	22 Jan 1947	9 Feb 1948	Yin	Fire	Pig
1948	10 Feb 1948	28 Jan 1949	Yang	Earth	Rat
1949	29 Jan 1949	16 Feb 1950	Yin	Earth	Ox

1950	17 Feb 1950	5 Feb 1951	Yang	Metal	Tiger
1951	6 Feb 1951	26 Jan 1952	Yin	Metal	Hare
1952	27 Jan 1952	13 Feb 1953	Yang	Water	Dragon
1953	14 Feb 1953	2 Feb 1954	Yin	Water	Snake
1954	3 Feb 1954	23 Jan 1955	Yang	Wood	Horse
1955	24 Jan 1955	11 Feb 1956	Yin	Wood	Goat
1956	12 Feb 1956	30 Jan 1957	Yang	Fire	Monkey
1957	31 Jan 1957	17 Feb 1958	Yin	Fire	Cockerel
1958	18 Feb 1958	7 Feb 1959	Yang	Earth	Dog
1959	8 Feb 1959	27 Jan 1960	Yin	Earth	Pig
1960	28 Jan 1960	14 Feb 1961	Yang	Metal	Rat
1961	15 Feb 1961	4 Feb 1962	Yin	Metal	Ox
1962	5 Feb 19622	4 Jan 1963	Yang	Water	Tiger
1963	25 Jan 1963	12 Feb 1964	Yin	Water	Hare
1964	13 Feb 1964	1 Feb 1965	Yang	Wood	Dragon
1965	2 Feb 1965	20 Jan 1966	Yin	Wood	Snake
1966	21 Jan 1966	8 Feb 1967	Yang	Fire	Horse
1967	9 Feb 1967	29 Jan 1968	Yin	Fire	Goat
1968	30 Jan 1968	16 Feb 1969	Yang	Earth	Monkey

1969	17 Feb 1969	5 Feb 1970	Yin	Earth	Cockerel
1970	6 Feb 1970	26 Jan 1971	Yang	Metal	Dog
1971	27 Jan 1971	15 Jan 1972	Yin	Metal	Pig
1972	16 Jan 1972	2 Feb 1973	Yang	Water	Rat
1973	3 Feb 1973	22 Jan 1974	Yin	Water	Ox
1974	23 Jan 1974	10 Feb 1975	Yang	Wood	Tiger
1975	11 Feb 1975	30 Jan 1976	Yin	Wood	Hare
1976	31 Jan 1976	17 Feb 1977	Yang	Fire	Dragon
1977	18 Feb 1977	6 Feb 1978	Yin	Fire	Snake
1978	7 Feb 1978	27 Jan 1979	Yang	Earth	Horse
1979	28 Jan 1979	15 Feb 1980	Yin	Earth	Goat
1980	16 Feb 1980	4 Feb 1981	Yang	Metal	Monkey
1981	5 Feb 1981	24 Jan 1982	Yin	Metal	Cockerel
1982	25 Jan 1982	12 Feb 1983	Yang	Water	Dog
1983	13 Feb 1983	1 Feb 1984	Yin	Water	Pig
1984	2 Feb 1984	19 Feb 1985	Yang	Wood	Rat
1985	20 Feb 1985	8 Feb 1986	Yin	Wood	Ox
1986	9 Feb 1986	29 Jan 1987	Yang	Fire	Tiger
1987	29 Jan 19871	6 Feb 1988	Yin	Fire	Hare

1988	17 Feb 1988	5 Feb 1989	Yang	Earth	Dragon
1989	6 Feb 1989	26 Jan 1990	Yin	Earth	Snake
1990	27 Jan 1990	14 Feb 1991	Yang	Metal	Horse
1991	15 Feb 1991	3 Feb 1992	Yin	Metal	Goat
1992	4 Feb 1992	22 Jan 1993	Yang	Water	Monkey
1993	23 Jan 1993	9 Feb 1994	Yin	Water	Cockerel
1994	10 Feb 1994	30 Jan 1995	Yang	Wood	Dog
1995	31 Jan 1995	18 Feb 1996	Yin	Wood	Pig
1996	19 Feb 1996	7 Feb 1997	Yang	Fire	Rat
1997	8 Feb 1997	27 Jan 1998	Yin	Fire	Ox
1998	28 Jan 1998	15 Feb 1999	Yang	Earth	Tiger
1999	16 Feb 1999	4 Feb 2000	Yin	Earth	Hare
2000	5 Feb 2000	23 Jan 2001	Yang	Metal	Dragon
2001	24 Jan 2001	11 Feb 2002	Yin	Metal	Snake
2002	12 Feb 2002	31 Jan 2003	Yang	Water	Horse
2003	1 Feb 2003	21 Jan 2004	Yin	Water	Goat
2004	22 Jan 2004	8 Feb 2005	Yang	Wood	Monkey
2005	9 Feb 2005	28 Jan 2006	Yin	Wood	Cockerel
2006	29 Jan 2006	17 Feb 2007	Yang	Fire	Dog
2007	18 Feb 2007	6 Feb 2008	Yin	Fire	Pig

Now you know which is your animal, you need to know where that animal 'feels' best. Again it is based on compass directions with each of the animals being assigned to a particular direction. The charts overleaf list for each animal:

- its Chinese name

- its assigned compass direction

- the animal's element (this is its natural element and not your element)

- a key word to describe that animal's particular characteristic

- its 'best' time of day

- the month that the animal 'rules'

- its Western astrological equivalent

	Rat	Ox	Tiger
Chinese name	Tzu	Ch'ou	Yin
Compass point	North	NNE	ENE
Element	Water	Metal	Fire
Characteristic	Promotion	Travel	Energy
Best time	11pm–1am	1–3am	3–5am
Month	December	January	February
Western Zodiac	Sagittarius	Capricorn	Aquarius

	Hare	Dragon	Snake
Chinese name	Mao	Chen	Ssu
Compass point	East	ESE	SSE
Element	Wood	Water	Metal
Characteristic	Marriage	Sexuality	Children
Best time	5–7am	7–9am	9–11am
Month	March	April	May
Western Zodiac	Pisces	Aries	Taurus

	Horse	Goat	Monkey
Chinese name	Wu	Wei	Shen
Compass point	South	SSW	WSW
Element	Fire	Wood	Water
Characteristic	Property	Family	Money
Best time	11am-1pm	1–3pm	3–5pm
Month	June	July	August
Western Zodiac	Gemini	Cancer	Leo

	Cockerel	Dog	Pig
Chinese name	Yu	Hsu	Hai
Compass point	West	WNW	NNW
Element	Metal	Fire	Wood
Characteristic	Longevity	Friends	Happiness
Best time	5–7pm	7–9pm	9–11pm
Month	September	October	November
Western Zodiac	Virgo	Libra	Scorpio

These could be laid out onto your pa kwa so you can
see how they all fit in.

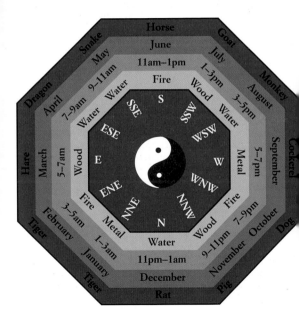

Summary

In the next section – Feng Shui In Action – we will look at how you can actually implement changes within your home to correct any 'bad' feng shui you have. But first we need to recap, just so you know where we've got to.

- Ch'i is energy which flows continually from yin to yang, from yang to yin (*see p.15–18*).

- Yang and yin are the two principles of all things – light and dark, spirit and matter, day and night, heat and cold, north and south (*see p.12–13*).

- The compass directions are important as they each have a different type of ch'i which affects various areas of our life (*see p.16*).

- These areas are known as enrichments and there are eight of them. You need to know where they fit into your own home and may need to draw up a ground plan and work them out using the pa kwa (*see p.30–32*).

- You need to know which of the eight types of house you have – from the eight possible directions your house could face in and this is set by the direction your front door faces (*see p.33–35*).

- Each area can be adversely affected by negative ch'i – *sha* (*see p.8*).

- There are eight remedies to correct the flow of any bad ch'i (*see p.34–40*).

- Each of the remedies has a particular enrichment in which it works best (*see p.41*).

- You only attempt to correct the flow of ch'i when you feel a particular area of your life needs improving. Feng shui is a way of making changes. We only need to make changes if there is something wrong.

FENG SHUI IN ACTION

Feng Shui and the Landscape

If we work in an office block or factory there is usually little we can do to radically alter the feng shui of the entire building – not without the permission of our employers anyway – but our home is so much easier to rectify.

If we start our day at home and our living environment is pleasant, harmonious and has good feng shui, we will be more ready to take on the challenges of the world. Once we step out from our front door we are a little at the mercy of whatever fate will throw at us; but our home is our personal domain and we can make it as balanced and tranquil as we require.

KEY AREAS TO CHECK

There are some important areas of our immediate surroundings that we need to examine when we are applying feng shui to our homes. These are listed overleaf and if I explain each in order, it will make it easier to remember then when you begin to consider each in your own environment.

KEY AREAS TO CHECK IN YOUR SURROUNDINGS

- Mountains (**Shan**)
- Surroundings (**Hsueh**)
- Water (**Shui**)
- Wind (**Feng**)
- Trees (**Liu**)
- Dwelling (**Chai**)
- Inside (**Fang**)
- Ourselves (**Jen hsin**)

Of course, if you are building a house on a new plot then you can exercise greater control over each of these elements than if, like most people, you move into a house that is already built. Nevertheless, you can still apply the principles outlined on the following pages either to check the suitability of a house you may be considering moving to or to improve the feng shui of your present home. It is also worth remembering that sites and their surroundings are often subject to change as areas develop and evolve. You should keep aware of such developments that may affect your home and act accordingly.

MOUNTAINS

The principles relating to *shan* – mountains – can still apply even if, as town- or city-dwellers here in the West, often we do not live close to mountains, or even hills. If this is so, we can instead consider any tall buildings near us as 'mountains'. Like mountain or hills, their massive presence can overpower our ch'i. To counter this, concave and convex mirrors can invert their image and so negate the effect of their powerful ch'i. Similarly, their reflection in a bowl of water will 'flatten' their image and similarly lessen their dominance.

Tall buildings, like mountains, have powerful ch'i that can overwhelm the ch'i in smaller buildings close to them

Any tall buildings close to you should, ideally, be in the Tortoise and Dragon areas, i.e. to the north and east *(see p.18)*. If they are not, you will have to flatten them: place mirrors in your Phoenix and Tiger areas (south and west)to make flat areas . Also small mirrors placed face out in the window are effective remedies.

SURROUNDINGS

The principles relating to *hsueh* – surroundings – means checking the areas in the immediate vicinity of your home for good or bad feng shui. You should know, preferably before you move into a new house, just what are the neighbours like? Consider also whether there are any unsightly buildings quite close to you. Stand outside your house and turn towards the four cardinal points of the compass to assess the area and the environment surrounding your property.

You also need to be aware of the four types of ch'i that will be directed at your home from each of these directions:

- **Yang ch'i** – *nourishing ch'i* from the south
- **Sheng ch'i** – *growing ch'i* from the east
- **T'sang ch'i** – *hidden ch'i* from the north
- **Sha ch'i** – *disruptive ch'i* from the west

Let's consider some of the options that may be facing you in each of the directions and what remedies can be taken to lessen the effects of bad feng shui.

SOUTH

Stand with your back to the side of the house that faces south. If you find yourself looking at a particularly unpleasant view, for example, of an abattoir or a factory belching smoke or a prison, this would seriously diminish the nourishing yang ch'i coming from this direction. Consider also the side of the house facing south; does it contain your main entrance or is it a blank wall? Fortunately, if it is blank then any unpleasant ch'i flowing towards it will not do too much damage.

EAST

The east is where the stimulating sheng ch'i is coming from, the ch'i that gives you your creative energy. What's there? Another unpleasant view of factories and industrial estates? Or a splendid view of the country-side? Which would you prefer?

NORTH

Now consider the t'sang ch'i, hidden ch'i, coming from the north. Ideally, this should undulate down towards you from tortoise hills in a gentle embracing way. What have you got there? Hopefully, protective hills or at least higher ground because if the area to your north is large and flat, there is nowhere for the nurturing ch'i to accumulate and roll down towards you from.

WEST

From the west comes the sha ch'i which as we've already said is disruptive and unpredictable. Some people even go so far sometimes as to say it's dangerous and destructive and they would even paint all west-facing windows black to eliminate any danger from this direction. We probably don't need to go that far but we should certainly pay attention to the environment from where your sha ch'i is coming from and importantly, how it is then getting into your home.

If it's entering through the front door then you need to deflect it fairly emphatically using the largest mirror you can on the inside wall immediately opposite the door. This deflects the sha straight back out again. For a back door, a smaller mirror or wind chimes are effective in breaking up the sha as it enters. If this door isn't used very often then deflect the sha coming towards it is less important.

Consider also any windows that open to the west. Sha entering by this route can be deflected if you use small glass balls hung in the window area that spin round and reflect the light.

Consider also what structures are in the west. Whatever is there, imagine it as energy – energy that is going to be amplified simply because it's in the west. Tiger ch'i is disruptive, erratic and potentially

Glass decorations placed in a west-facing window will deflect the disruptive sha ch'i

dangerous. If you've got anything stressful there such as an industrial area, prison, factory, police station, funeral parlour or even a butcher's shop, you have to imagine the ch'i coming towards you and bringing with it any stress, pain, emotional upsets and distress. Because of this, the area to the west of any house you may be considering buying should be examined carefully before you decide. Most of your problems will emanate from this direction and so it needs careful consideration before you make any major decisions.

TERRACES

If you live in a terrace then the ch'i coming from your neighbours is important. If you live in a semi-detached or terraced house then obviously you can't go outside and check all the compass directions with your back to each of your walls. However, you can go to the end of the row of houses or terrace and check out each of compass directions from there.

TOWER BLOCKS

If you live in a high rise building or block of flats you have the added difficulty of having to consider what ch'i is rising from below. Perhaps you live above a shop; if so, is the ch'i filtering up through your floors from it likely to be positive or negative? The Chinese, for example, would never live above a butcher's shop but would have no qualms about living above a bank.

BASEMENTS

On the other hand, living in a basement needs special attention because of what is above you. Again it may be shops or other flats. In general, the Chinese feel that any place that may have generated emotional distress such as hospitals, police stations, prisons, etc. give off a particular type of ch'i called *fan ch'i*, which can be translated as 'offensive ch'i'. This type of ch'i can be quite harmful because it carries with it the same emotional distress from its source to you.

FENG SHUI AND HARMONY

A lot of feng shui is intuitive work: you have to look yourself and feel whether the energy is right. Yet a lot of feng shui is also common sense. If every time you open your front door you are confronted with a dreadful view you are bound to feel worse than if you look out on a wonderful vista of countryside, streams and beautiful hills. Your quality of life improves with the quality of your horizons. Feng shui is also about taking responsibility. We all choose where we live. Maybe feng shui is about making that choice. We can improve it but ultimately you may have to move if you come to realise that where and how you live is adversely affecting your emotional and spiritual horizons.

Some people however can resist negative forces better than others. You're perfectly entitled to live opposite a factory if you choose, just be aware that you're making that choice.

We need to look for harmony in our lives, to seek out the natural and the nurturing. If we choose to live in an inner city surrounded by derelict buildings, busy polluted roads and millions of other people then we are going to feel the effects that all that negative ch'i generates. If we choose to live in the countryside in quiet tranquil surroundings with beautiful views then we will benefit. Obviously there has to be, as in all things, a question of balance. There will always be a time in our lives when we need the excitement and stimulation a city offers and a time when we need to get away from it all. Judging when those times are, is up to you. Only you can tell when you have had enough and need to move. A lot of people however don't even think about the alternatives. Feng shui is about seeking that balance, that harmony.

WATER AND WIND

If you don't enjoy the advantages of living near rivers, streams or other water features then you have to introduce this element to your life yourself. This is why aquariums are so popular in Chinese communities around the world.

Water carries ch'i as well as being a soothing element of our environment. If there are rivers and streams close by, look at the way they transport ch'i towards us. Beneficial ch'i likes to meander whereas the disruptive sha prefers to travel in straight lines. So, if the river heads straight for your home or is a concrete-banked canal, it carries sha, whereas if it meanders happily around your house or is a gently gurgling stream, it will be a bringer of beneficial ch'i.

If your house overlooks a large body of water such as a lake or reservoir, then you have to give these special consideration. Large bodies of water, even large ponds, accumulate ch'i which can be overwhelming. This is a particular problem if it lies to the west. A lake here would store sha in large quantities and would almost certainly be an extraordinarily powerful force that would erupt unpredictably. This is both good feng shui and common sense. Feng shui says it's an accumulation of energy; common sense says it's an accumulation of water which could flood in times of heavy rain.

If the lake is to the north then the t'sang ch'i coming from this direction could make you very sleepy indeed.

Large bodies of water represent considerable reservoirs of energy

We need water in the home and using mirrors to bring watery views inside is a very positive remedy: the sight and sound of water moving naturally can be most beneficial and soothing.

TREES

A direct translation of *liu* would actually be 'willow' which is the tree most often represented in traditional Chinese landscape paintings (known as shan-shui). Liu – trees – can also be more broadly interpreted as 'garden'. The feng shui of gardens is a large subject in its own right and will be discussed later (*see* p.121). Buildings represent the yang element of the landscape and, correspondingly, trees are the yin. Both are essential for harmony in our environment. The shan-shui artists follow a ratio of 3 to 2 in composing their paintings: three yang elements to two yin. For this, hills as yang and hollows as yin. In any panorama three fifths should be yang, the sky, and two fifths yin, the landscape and yin trees can be used to balance any excess of yang buildings or yang hills.

DWELLING

This refers to the feng shui of a specific building: the entrance, each room, its windows and doors, etc. This is explored more fully later (*see pp.98–114*).

OURSELVES

The people who live in a property are the most important elements in it and it's pointless expending our energies getting the feng shui of our home right if we ourselves are not in harmony. Getting the feng shui right can make quite a difference but we also need to sort out our own personal feng shui. We are the focus of all that good ch'i and we need to ensure that we put it to good use in how we interact with those around us. Essentially, we need to be as balanced as our home.

Types of Sites

SHAPE

You should consider carefully the overall shape of any plot of land – including buildings – that you own or are preparing to buy. Irregular-shaped plots are considered to have poor feng shui whilst regular-shaped plots are better. The best shape of all for a site would be the octagon (although this is perhaps rarely encountered) followed by the circle, square and oblong.

If the shape is irregular there will be 'missing' areas from the eight enrichments (*see p.30*) and if they are not completely missing, then the particular enrichments will be lacking in breadth and dimension.

Obviously, you need all eight areas for your life to be in balance and working well. Areas that are cut off or shortened will mean you will not be able to live to the fullest of your potential.

Rectangular, circular and octagonal: ideal plot shapes

Irregular-shaped plots have poor feng shui because certain enrichment areas will be diminished or missing completely

WATER COURSES

If you live near rivers or canals you need to take into consideration how the water will affect the feng shui of your home. Large bodies of water have their own particular ch'i and it can be very powerful. Long straight canals funnel ch'i too strongly and if the canal is pointing directly at your home it will make you feel exhausted and tired. Gentle meandering rivers on the other hand are beneficial and bring healthy ch'i towards you. If the river flows away from your house, so will the ch'i.

A gentle flowing river is an auspicious feature in a landscape bringing healthy ch'i

RULES FOR WATER COURSES

- Beware of buying a property with water courses to the rear

- Generally, the best place for any water to be is in front of any building

FAVOURABLE WATER-COURSE SITES

Where water flows converge near the house

With a pond to the front of the house

Where the flow 'embraces' the house

UNFAVOURABLE WATER-COURSE SITES

*Where the
flow divides*

*Where the
flow is directly
at the house*

*Where the flow
'threatens' the house*

*Where a large body of
water is to the rear*

BUILDING SHAPES

As with plot shape so building shape is also important.
The more irregular the shape, the worse the feng shui;

the more regular the better the feng shui. Building extensions to existing buildings is fraught with danger as it alters the shape of the house so fundamentally that it should not be considered unless it fills an otherwise empty enrichment area. Extensions should fill a gap in such areas, not add to them, unless you feel a particular lack of some enrichment in your life. A word of caution: simply building on an extension to add to your wealth area doesn't work!

ROOF SHAPES

Roof shapes are also important and you want to look for as normal a shape as possible. Anything quirky or odd will be considered to have poor feng shui. In

---

ROOF SHAPES

Unfavourable roof shapes are:

1 Irregular

2 Uneven

3 Flat

4 Sloping continuously from one side of the building to the other.

Favourable roof shapes are:

1 Regularly shaped

2 Proportional

China the roofs are curved to allow the ch'i to flow harmoniously – and to allow the rain to flow off as well.

ROADS

If roads channel ch'i, it makes sense to use this to our advantage. Roads aimed directly at our home will channel the ch'i too quickly. The Chinese refer to this as 'killing ch'i' because it directs too much ch'i at us, too quickly. Even more serious is what is known as 'arrowed killing ch'i' where two or more roads form a point or arrow-head aimed at our home.

Arrowed killing ch'i is one of the worst landscape features affecting home owners

If your home is faced with an arrowed killing ch'i it can make you defensive, even paranoid. You need to hang a mirror facing outwards to deflect the ch'i. The best type of mirrors are octagonal ones that reflect the shape of the pa kwa. These can be hard to get hold of so you can use ordinary square or oblong ones – these are fine for the purposes of deflecting ch'i. Even better would be a round one. However, make sure it is completely flat, rather than concave or convex mirrors – these should be used primarily for reducing the height of overpowering tower blocks (mountains). Alternatively, you could highly polish any metal fittings on your door.

The ideal site is one where the road runs across the front of your home – and as near to the corner that you can be the better. Living on a main road has draw backs since the cars going past quickly will draw away the ch'i, leaving your home depleted and lifeless. Ideally, the road should be quiet, gentle, slightly curving towards your home and tree lined although having all such components present in a single location would be rather rare.

CORNER PROPERTIES

If you have a corner site you have to pay some attention to your main entrance. The preferred location would be for it to cut across the corner.

The ideal position for the entrance to a corner property

Feng Shui and the Home

Before we start checking the individual rooms and features of your home there are a few points you should consider. Good feng shui means adopting a zero tolerance philosophy. In New York, this is known as the broken window syndrome, since it has been observed that if an apartment building gets one broken window and it is not repaired or replaced immediately, then within a very short space of time there is a general outbreak of vandalism leaving the whole building with broken windows, rubbish spilt everywhere and so on. If, on the other hand, the window is repaired or replaced immediately then the building retains its good character. This is how it should be with your own home. If you repair damage at once the ch'i remains bright and healthy. If you allow disrepair to creep in then the ch'i deteriorates quickly. This goes for decoration, tidying up, maintenance and cleaning. For feng shui purposes, the only method is to do it at once before it gets worse.

A TEN-POINT PLAN

If you are experiencing any problems connected with any of the eight enrichments (see p.30), it is always useful to have a plan to check mentally the state of your house or office in order to see if there are areas where you can take steps to improve the situation. Listed

below are ten key areas that you should look at. The
points are in no particular order of importance; all
should be checked regularly, although perhaps paying
particular attention to the first point – clutter – would
have the most immediate benefits. These things should
be done before implementing any specific remedies.

1   Clutter

2   Life

3   Windows

4   Heating

5   Lighting/Mirrors

6   Drainage

7   Doors

8   Electrics

9   Colour

10 Paths

Let's look at each of these in turn, and remember the
following are only tips and suggestions – nothing with
feng shui is set in concrete. You may find that some of
these don't apply, or you have different ideas about
them – that's fine. Do whatever you have to do to make

your life flow smoothly, successfully and satisfyingly. If you experience problems then you need to make changes. If everything is going well, then perhaps it's best to leave well alone – as they say, *if it ain't broke, don't fix it.*

CLUTTER

We all collect clutter – there's no avoiding the stuff. It materialises around us like dust under the sofa. Whatever we do, clutter will sneak into our lives and homes. The only thing you can do is be very strict about yourself and clear it out from time to time. Have you ever looked in your kitchen drawers? What have you got there? Old plastic carrier bags? Bits of string you've

A priority improving the feng shui in your home should be to remove or minimise mess and untidiness

saved and know full well you're never going to use?
Whatever it is, throw it away. If you have saved bits and
pieces and haven't used them to date, then throw them
away – the chances are you're never going to use them.

Check your cupboards,
especially the one under the
stairs, and while you're at it
check the garage. The garage
is a bit like our subconscious:
we can't see it so assume it's
fine. Well, it's probably not.
This is the place we collect all
the junk that tells us about
how our life has been in the
past – pots of old half-used
paint; rolls of carpet we'll
never need; broken tools and
machinery that will never get
fixed and have probably been
replaced by now with ones
that do work; toys left over
from when the children were
young and we can't bear to throw away. It's all clutter.
There's nothing for it but to throw it all away if you
want the ch'i to flow smoothly and well around and
through your home. And how long is it since you
checked the attic or under the bed?

Old suitcases on top of the wardrobe? Boxes of old

clothes and shoes on the landing? Chest of drawers full of last year's clothes. No, we're not being fashion conscious here, merely clutter-less. If clothes don't fit, are worn out, need repairing, look dreadful, have gone out of fashion, no longer suit you, whatever, there really is no alternative – throw them away or better still make them up into a big bag and take them down to your local charity shop. Boy George, the pop singer, did this recently and admits to sending 40 bags of clothing, in a single year, to the charity Oxfam. How many could you send?

Don't ignore the emotional clutter as well. Clear out your head from time to time. Throw away all those old love letters, photographs of old loves who you can't even remember any more, particularly anything that reminds you of anyone you have had problems with or carry any resentment towards.

In the office you can strip out your files from time to time. If you haven't looked at a piece of paper for three months or more, the chances are you'll never look at it again. Obviously, in some offices there are various official documents that you can't throw away for legal reasons, such as the Inland Revenue material. For these, why not store them somewhere else. Perhaps down in the basement?

Throw away old magazines, newspapers, envelopes and brochures. Every now and again pull out units in the

kitchen, if it's physically possible, and clean behind
them. You'd be surprised how much clutter collects
behind a washing machine or fridge. Make sure no dust
collects under your bed. Carpets should be vacuumed
regularly and rugs taken out into the garden and beaten
from time to time.

Check what you're
keeping on your book-
shelves as well. We all
have an amazing
tendency to keep and
collect books that will
never be read again and
yet we just can't bear to
throw them away. Find
somewhere to store
them and allow the ch'i
to circulate freely.

Check what lurks above shelves and cupboards as well.
If cobwebs can collect dust and dead flies then they can
collect ch'i. If a spider has finished with a web and
moved on to a new one, what are you saving the old
one for?

LIFE

You are life – you are the *jen* in the centre of your
home. But is that enough? Feng shui suggests that to be

in tune with nature we need to bring nature inside with us – to remind us of something bigger going on in our lives than just getting up and going to work. Fill your home with plants: pot plants, house plants, bonsai trees, climbers, vines, ivy, herbs on window sills,

whatever takes your fancy. Plants in pots are easy to maintain, easy to replace if they start looking a bit tatty, easy to look after if we go away a lot (you just need a friend and some water), easy for colour, life, interest and friendliness. A home without life is too stark and sterile.

Cut flowers are a bit frowned on in feng shui as they are full of dying ch'i leaking away – and it leaks into your home. If you simply must have cut flowers, change the water every day – and throw them away when they're dead. Also, any dead pot plants must be thrown away and replaced immediately. Similarly, dried flowers aren't really a good idea as they merely collect dust and should be thrown away.

Carefully select the pots you put your plants in – they should be made of natural materials – terracotta or stoneware. You should try to avoid plastic if you can. The colours of the pots should be checked to make sure they harmonise with the rest of the colour scheme. It's all too easy to just not notice a simple pot and yet it can throw a room's decor completely.

Plants with long pointed leaves aren't recommended. It's better to have nice round leaves that look like money. Dead-head any flowers as soon as they have withered.

Remember that it isn't only plants that can bring life into a home – why not think about a cat or a dog or mice, hamsters, birds, lizards, even stick insects? Getting a cat curled up on a cushion is a good way of introducing life into an area that needs remedying. Of course the trick is getting them to stay still…

And don't forget the best of all feng shui remedies –
fish. Make sure you always have an odd number and
keep the aquarium in your wealth enrichment to
promote money and income.

WINDOWS

Keep the curtains pulled well back from the windows
to allow maximum light to enter and make sure you
don't have any windows un-curtained at night. For feng
shui purposes, an exposed window looking out onto
the black night is considered a very bad omen indeed.

If you want blinds at your windows they should be
made of natural materials if possible; wood is good, as
is cotton fabric but try to avoid plastics if you can.
Watch out for the colours of blinds since as the ch'i
filters through it will take on the resonance of the blind
colour. This may be good if you want that colour quality in a particular room.

Curtains that just hang down limply either side of a
window aren't considered very good feng shui. They

WINDOWS TIP

- Keep them clean at all times to allow the free
  passage of ch'i to an dfrom a room

should have a little swag or curve to them. And ideally they should reach to the floor. When they're drawn open, they should be tied back on either side so they hang in graceful folds. And allow more material for your curtains than you'd think you'd need. Too much is preferable to too little. When the curtains are drawn together at night there should be masses of fabric hanging in pleats and folds rather than something that looks as if it just fits if drawn tightly enough together.

CURTAINS TIP

- Curtains should match the seasons as well – heavy drapes for the winter and lighter, finer fabrics for the summer. In any case, it's good to take your curtains down twice a year and clean them.

Curtains should be capable of being drawn and opened easily – if you've got to pull hard on them then there's something blocking the flow of energy. Examine the track that they move on. Ideally, it should be made of natural materials. A wooden pole with rings is good, while bamboo is even better. Plastic tracking isn't really ideal.

Windows should be capable of being opened if that's what they were intended to do. Any that are stuck up with paint should be freed up. Keep windows well painted – this isn't feng shui, it's home maintenance – they last longer if they're painted. Check the colours of any woodwork on windows on the outside of the house and make sure it harmonises with the rest of the house.

HEATING

When you've finished with your wood-burning stove or open fire for the winter then clear out the ashes and throw them away, and have the chimney swept immediately, rather than at the last minute just before you light the fire again for the first time in the autumn.

If you have central heating be aware that the rumble of water in radiators, pumps, boilers lighting up and the creak of metal as radiators and pipes cool down or heat up all bring sound into your home – and it may affect any sound remedies you're using.

Heaters, especially electric ones, should be as discreet as possible. If you can hide them, so much the better.

In an ideal home there would always be an open fire. If, because of local smoke regulations or some other reason, you can't have one then maybe you can get away with an imitation one but it must be realistic. Those old fashioned ones which relied on a single light bulb with a bit of coloured plastic aren't really suitable at all. Modern ones using gas to give a 'living flame' effect can be difficult to distinguish from the real thing.

Electric fan heaters that blow hot air do really weird things to the ch'i in a room and they should be used only if there is no other heating solution. A convector heater is a better option. Be aware that lights, computers, candles, stereos, ovens, cookers, any electrical equipment, all generate heat and as heat rises so does the ch'i. A very slow moving ceiling fan can help to push the ch'i back down into the room and it stops you feeling too drained. Ceiling fans

Every home should have one

are also very good movement remedies.

Any heating and ventilation ducts should be cleaned regularly, and extractor fans serviced at the right time. Keep it all clean and functioning properly and the ch'i can circulate well.

LIGHTING

All lighting should be subtle. Any harsh lights should be got rid of. Try to avoid shades that let you see down inside them – and hence see the bulb. Lights should do just that – light up things to enable you to see better – but they shouldn't be obvious. White light can be a strain on the eyes. Daylight bulbs are better. Lamps should throw gentle pools of light rather act as spotlights, although in a kitchen there may be a case for them. Overhead lights, ideally, should be on dimmer switches so you can regulate how much light they give out.

You don't have to restrict yourself to electric lights. In certain circumstances, candles can give out just as much light which is also softer and much more gentle on the eyes. Oil lamps are also more natural and give a very soft glow while firelight can be very soothing.

We are so used to electric light that we barely consider any alternatives. We need to look closely at what we want the lighting for. If we need task lighting, to read by for example, then obviously brightness is a main requirement and electric light will most likely be necessary. But when we are considering a room's ambient or general lighting then we should certainly look at the full range of options.

LIGHTING TIP

- if you can see any bare light bulbs then this is poor feng shui

MIRRORS

Mirrors are for reflecting and looking into, so how can we do this if they are misted up, dirty, aged and cracked? Keep mirrors clean and bright. Mirrors, if they're the sort you look into rather than being used specifically as remedies, should be at head height. That may sound obvious but so many people have mirrors that are too low or too high. But what about smaller people? Easy. Angle the mirrors so they lean slightly away from the wall at the top and then everybody can see themselves clearly in them. Angled mirrors are also very flattering which is why many clothes shops have theirs angled – they make you look several pounds lighter.

Mirrors used as remedies should be small and discreet. If you can get hold of the octagonal pa kwa mirrors which have the eight trigrams on them, so much the better. To deflect sha, mirrors should be placed so they face outwards. To channel ch'i inside the house you'll have to angle them so they do their job properly.

Avoid mirrors that have pictures engraved or printed on them. Bad taste is also bad feng shui. Oval mirrors are good, especially if they have ornate wooden surrounds. Mirrors should be the highest quality you can afford. And they make good remedies for when you need to see behind you. If you have to have your back to the door in an office or the kitchen you can position a mirror so that you can always see if there is someone behind you – a very important aspect of feng shui.

MIRROR TIP

- have a large mirror angled on a wall so it reflects a beautiful view into the room when you're sitting in your favourite chair, or lying in bed, or relaxing in the bath

---

DRAINAGE

The drains are the digestive system of your house. Get them blocked up and the waste ch'i can't be eliminated – and it will stagnate as will any water trapped in blocked pipes. Any outside drainage systems should be regularly inspected for blockages and if any are found they should be cleared at once. Inspection covers to drains should be firmly in place, and any that are cracked or broken should be replaced.

Clear out the gutters and get rid of the winter's leaves that invariably collect there. Make sure your garden drains well – pools of muddy water lying on the lawn aren't helpful. The word 'sha' actually means 'noxious vapour' and it describes the sort of mist you get off stagnant water from neglected pools. If you have a pond in the garden this should be drained and cleaned every now and again to avoid stagnant water, mud and the build-up of too much weed.

Any washing-up equipment that is past it's best should be replaced, this includes scourers, cloths, wire brushes, pan cleaners and cleaning fluids. Washing up bowls should be replaced regularly and, ideally, there should be at least two – one for plates and one for food items.

Make sure all sinks are kept clean, drain well, and have no leaky fittings

Any sinks or baths that are chipped, cracked, or broken in any way should be replaced.

Make sure the area under sinks, particularly in kitchens, is kept clear of clutter, and clean. This is both good feng shui and a good safety procedure to keep chemicals out of children's reach.

Check that all taps can be turned off completely and that nothing leaks or drips. Lavatories should be kept with both the seat and lid down. Sinks and baths should be disinfected regularly and all stains and marks removed from enamel surfaces. Any chrome work on taps and shower attachments should be kept brightly polished.

Any cold water storage tanks in attics or roof spaces should be inspected and covered if open. Hot water systems should be checked for leaks, rusting or blockages.

DOORS

Doors are like the nervous system of a house – if they stick they will irritate and cause tension. They allow communication to happen so they should be able to be freely opened and closed and easy to pass through. Double doors which open in the middle should have both halves opened at the same time rather than trying to squeeze through one half that is too small.

Keep doors for the purpose for which they are intended – which isn't as hat stands, coat racks or the storage of your dressing gown. Doors are for opening and allowing fresh ch'i to enter. And for closing to stop ch'i leaving. If you have a space where there used to be a door and it isn't there any longer, but the surround is, then try to replace the door. If you have a door that isn't used any more it is probably best to remove it and partition the area off properly.

Oil hinges and locks regularly to eliminate any squeaks or rattles thus ensuring they open silently and don't stick. Doors should be kept well painted – especially any outside ones – and avoid over harsh gloss paints, a matt, satin or silk finish is best. This avoids too much reflection which turns the door into a giant mirror, perhaps in a place where you didn't want a mirror remedy. Outside doors should be painted in sympathy with the rest of the house.

Stable doors can be beneficial in that you can open the top half to let in air in the summer much like a window. But make sure that neither half sticks, they should be able to be opened smoothly and effortlessly.

Any door fittings in the way of handles, knockers, letter boxes and bolts should be kept polished and clean.

ELECTRICS

Electric pollution is present in most homes, affecting our nerves and making us feel tense and irritable. In our houses and workplaces we spend long hours surrounded by powerful 'ring mains' circuits; these act as giant magnets which possibly have a detrimental effect on our health. Yet how many of us could live without such power, such energy, now? If we have to live with it we can at least make it our servant, instead of the other way round.

As technology spreads increasingly into every aspect of our daily existence so we get more electric pollution around us. We need to stop occasionally and take stock of the technology we are accumulating around us. Electrical appliances are powerful mechanical object remedies. When feng shui was first devised there were no electrical gadgets so there was no need to take them into account. Now however they have taken the first place as a remedy in our home and as such have become a curse rather than a cure. The secret it to try to eliminate them or at least to try to contain them or put them into areas where they will do the least harm.

Since ch'i likes to follow curving lines, what could be more attractive than electric cables – and what could be worse? Go round your house and just see how many electric cables you have snaking behind desks, down bedside tables, across work surfaces, across floors – and they all head in the same direction – downwards – with the result that that's where the ch'i ends up, on the floor. If you can hide the cables so much the better but this of course can be very difficult. You can at least secure them together neatly and pin them along the edge of the floor or tape them out of sight to the back of a cupboard or other piece of furniture. Don't forget all those telephone wires coiling across the floor.

Look at how the electricity cables come into your home. Check that the fuse box is in working order with no loose or broken wires; as far as is practicable, make sure it is discreet and hidden away.

Living near, or under, electricity pylons and substations is alleged to pose a considerable health hazard. If your house is in this position and it concerns you, then the only real remedy you can consider is to move away from the source of the problem.

Electricity pylons are impossible to remedy other than by avoiding their presence altogether

Colour

Feng shui is not interior decoration and no one can tell you what colours you should decorate your home in. However, it should be possible to find a colour scheme you like which also promotes good feng shui around your house.

The key to this is to choose colours that are suitable to your element and compass direction, based on which astrological animal you are (*see p. 50*). The tables below and overleaf indicate suitable colours for each sign.

COMPASS DIRECTIONS AND COLOUR

- **South**: strong reds
- **South east**: reds, terracottas, yellows
- **East**: strong greens
- **North east**: soft greens
- **North**: blues, blacks
- **North west**: off-whites
- **West**: whites, with warm (gold) highlights
- **South west**: browns, yellows

ELEMENTS AND COLOURS

- **Earth**: yellow and browns

- **Fire**: reds

- **Water**: blues

- **Metal**: white, silver, gold, pastels

- **Wood**: greens, blues

Which colour scheme to adopt also depends on which direction your house faces. For example, if your house faces north east and you're the element metal then you could combine soft greens with white and silver. Similarly, if you have a south-facing house and you're the element earth, you could use combinations of reds, oranges, yellows and browns, in this instance, terracotta would be a good colour for you.

You can also vary the colour of any enrichment depending on which compass direction it faces.

Colours can become cluttered very easily. In an ideal house you would probably avoid patterned fabrics and wallpapers as much as possible as they play havoc with ch'i. Use instead solid colours and simple colour

combinations. If you want
your walls to have texture
try using colour washes
and sponging effects as
they harmonise the ch'i
rather than distracting it.
It is also a very useful
personal input: you form
an intimate relationship
with your house if you
design and decorate it yourself
rather than buying something
someone else designed.

*The four 'lucky' colours
of red, white, black and
gold that are so loved
by the Chinese*

PATHS

The route to your front door may be more important
than you realise in feng shui terms. It brings the world
to you and brings you the dominant aspect of your personal ch'i. Go outside and stand at the end of the path
and face towards your house. What do you see? Be very
critical, very objective. Now look out at surroundings.
Do the two marry up? Are they in harmony with each
other? If not, why not? What will you do about it?

You need a clear route up to your front door, not too
straight, and not too curved. The path shouldn't funnel
or open out. Anything, like hedges or trees, that
obscures the path should be removed, pruned, clipped
or reshaped. If the path is obscured then so will both

the ch'i and your personal 'face' – your reputation and fame.

Avoid having to step over anything – or tripping up in the dark. Light the route so you and your visitors can see clearly which way to go.

House Features

Now that we've looked at the basic structure of the house and its setting, we can turn our attention to the individual rooms and features and what remedies can be applied to inauspicious arrangement or components in each. You can use any combination of the eight remedies available to improve the feng shui in your house. As we've discussed (*see p.41*), different remedies work to best effect in different circumstances, but however you choose to use them, remember that you can do no harm: you can only improve the feng shui because you are using natural cures. The worst you can do is keep things as they are.

FRONT DOOR

Consider what your main door looks like. Is it in proportion to its setting in the house? If it's too large then there is the risk that too much ch'i will be being allowed to escape each time it is opened. To prevent this, hang a wind chime close to it to reflect the ch'i back into the house.

FRONT DOOR TIPS

The exterior of the main door:

1 Should not face a lamp post or a tree

2 Should not face the direction of the driveway or path

The interior of the main door:

1 Should not face the back door

2 Should not face a blank interior wall or staircase

3 Should not face a bedroom, the kitchen or toilet

If the main door is too small, hanging mirrors either side of it will give the illusion of it being bigger than it is.

Consider also the direction your door faces and so the sort of ch'i it is letting in. Having established this, you can take the appropriate steps to counter any sha directed at it (*see p.34–41*).

ENTRANCE HALL

If your house has an entrance hall, rather than simply rush through it, you should view it as an area to collect yourself before you enter or leave the home proper. To put you in the correct frame of mind, it is important therefore that the hallway is as tranquil as possible.

THE STAIRCASE

Ch'i flows both up to the upper floors and also down from them via the staircase. If the stairs are too close to the front door then the ch'i will flow down and straight out, particularly if they directly face the door, leaving the upstairs rooms feeling drained and empty. The flow of ch'i can be broken up using a wind chime or even a well-positioned plant.

Stairs with bends in them can help the ch'i to flow well as it likes to curve and meander. However, too sharp or severe a bend will effectively block the ch'i. A mirror strategically placed at the bend of the staircase will remedy this.

A curving staircase is ideal for allowing ch'i to flow between floors

SPIRAL STAIRCASES

Spiral staircases create their own problems. If they have open treads then the ch'i will fall straight through, and the staircase will act as a drain. The best remedy is to fill in the treads. If this isn't practical then try placing a small mirror face up underneath the stairs to reflect some of the ch'i back upstairs.

Spiral staircases are a problem even without open treads: their perfect curves encourage the ch'i to move too quickly down them, leaving the upper floor drained. Any remedies therefore must aim to slow down the flow of ch'i on the stairs. Possibilities include growing a vine or other similar plants up the main central support or if that is impractical, then paint the stairwell pale green. Failing that, place a small mirror underneath them and perhaps also reinforce this with another remedy such as a wind chime hung half-way down the stairs.

The trick with stairs is to stand at the top and then at the bottom and imagine you are the ch'i. Ask yourself where you would flow, how quickly, what you would encounter and what would help you, then choose your remedies accordingly.

BATHROOMS/TOILETS

The Chinese believe that a toilet with its seat-lid left up will allow ch'i to drain away, therefore it is very important to keep the lid down. Also, try to ensure that the bathroom is not in your *wang ts'ai* area which covers your prosperity and wealth. If it is, the warning against leaving the seat-lid up is twice as dire. The bathroom door should be kept closed as much as possible and

Never leave the toilet seat up

hang a mirror on it facing outwards.

If you have a toilet which is separate from the bathroom, it should not face the door. However, this is often unavoidable and if so, you should try to have a window above the toilet itself, which you should keep bright and inviting. If the view is good, make it easy to see (people can always draw the curtains once they're in the room). If the view is poor, put a pot plant on the windowsill. If there is no window, hang a mirror above the toilet instead.

THE LIVING ROOM

As this is one principle rooms of any house, it is important to get its feng shui correct. Begin by checking which of the eight enrichments (*see p.30*) your living room falls into. For obvious reasons, being positioned in *an lu*, peace and happiness is auspicious but depending on your particular element, other enrichments might be more suitable; for example, fire types may prefer it to be in *ch'ang yin,* pleasure and indulgence.

LIVING ROOM TIP

- If your dining area or kitchen opens off the living room, try to prevent these being the first things seen when the door to the living room is opened. If possible, they should be screened with a plant-covered trellis or something similar.

Furniture should be arranged so that the 'honoured guest' position faces the door. The honoured guest position is usually the best one in the room: the most comfortable chair, the one affording the best view. This honoured guest position is usually the one we select for ourselves. Try to make sure it faces the door, in the same way you would with your desk in an office.

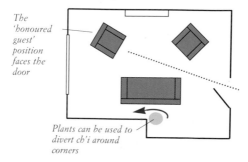

The 'honoured guest' position faces the door

Plants can be used to divert ch'i around corners

Be aware of corners and alcoves which can be 'dead' areas in a room as far as the flow of ch'i is concerned. As well as using colour and light to lift these areas, you can also place an aquarium or a pot plant there as a life remedy although make sure any plant has rounded leaves, rather than spiky ones. You can also use plants to soften sharp any corners jutting into the room, which could aggravate or disrupt the ch'i. Either place a tall plant in front of the corner, or attach a shelf higher up and train a trailing plant to cover the corner.

If your living room is not in the enrichment you would like it to be, and you can't swap your rooms around, introduce a remedy which would suit the enrichment you would like for your living room. For example, if you would like it in your social activities enrichment, choose remedies which would suit this. Sound remedies are the best for your friends and new beginnings enrichment, so put a chiming clock or a CD player in the living room to represent the friends and new beginnings enrichment.

Opposite is a reminder of the eight enrichments and the remedies which best suit each one:

FURNITURE LAYOUT

The layout of the seating in the living room is the most important aspect of the room. You should aim for the seating to create something as close to a circle, octagon

ENRICHMENTS AND REMEDIES

Enrichment	Remedy
Fame	Light
Health & happiness	Straight lines
Social activities	Stillness
Friends & new beginnings	Sound
Relationships	Movement
Children & family	Colour
Wisdom & experience	Mechanical device
Wealth	Life

or square as you can manage. It's likely that at least one wall will be taken up with a fireplace (the traditional focal point of the living room) or a television (the modern day focus) but the remaining seats should be arranged to avoid creating a line-up or corridor of chairs and sofas.

The living room should not be cluttered with furniture,

or the ch'i can't flow around it, so make sure the amount of furniture, and its size, suits the proportions of the room. A large mirror in the room, preferably above the fireplace, will help to create a feeling of space.

FOCUS POINT OF THE ROOM

The focal point of any Western living room was always the fireplace until television became commonplace. If you regard a fire as a movement remedy and a television as a mechanical remedy you can see that our living rooms may well be unbalanced and that we need to take steps to restore it.

One way of doing this is to avoid giving the television or other electrical appliances such as the hi fi positions of prominence in the room. These would be better housed out of sight in cabinets and watched only when needed. When they were not needed they could be discreetly hidden away. If it is not possible to enclose the television, then a good alternative would be to hide behind a small screen decorated to blend with the rest of the decor in the room.

The fireplace could take up its proper focal position in rooms once again. In some Mediterranean countries the fireplace is positioned in the corner of the room. This is sound feng shui as it adds a curve to the corner, allowing ch'i to circulate and also provides one side for the preferred octagonal arrangement of items in the room.

GOOD FENG SHUI FOR LIVING ROOMS

- Choose a suitable enrichment for your living room, or introduce the appropriate remedy for the enrichment you would like the room to fall in.

- Keep the living room light and bright, using colour, light and pot plants to remedy dark or sharp corners.

- Arrange the furniture to create a circle, square or octagon of seats, and avoid cluttering the room with too much furniture.

- Make sure you have an honoured guest position opposite the door.

- The room should be warm and cosy, with pictures and ornaments, but it should not be cluttered with children's toys or piles of old magazines.

THE DINING ROOM

As with living rooms, make sure the furniture in the dining room allows the ch'i to flow unhindered and harmoniously around the room. Once again, the honoured guest position should face the door. The door shouldn't open too close to any chairs. If possible, the table should incorporate the octagonal pa kwa shape if not in the shape of the table itself then as the place settings or the chair arrangements or even in the table decoration such as a tablecloth or centrepiece.

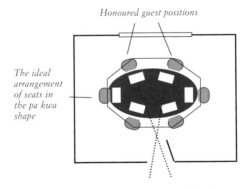

Honoured guest positions

The ideal arrangement of seats in the pa kwa shape

Make sure there is plenty of room to open the door and walk around the table and chairs without feeling cramped. If you can't do this, you need a smaller table. If this means you haven't room for all the friends you like to entertain, don't cram them into an over-full room or they'll all end up with indigestion! Change your arrangements so that you eat buffet style, or in the kitchen. Mirrors will help the room to feel larger;

they should be placed so they reflect the food on the table.

If the dining room is too close to the front door, people won't stay long after they've eaten. If you can't change the layout, at least keep the dining room door closed once the food is served.

GOOD FENG SHUI FOR DINING ROOMS

- Find the most suitable enrichment you can for the dining room.

- Focus on the table, which should be round, oval or octagonal.

- Don't overcrowd the room with furniture.

- Don't locate the dining room in sight of the front door.

THE BEDROOM

Given that we spend up to a third of our lives in the bedroom, we should give particular attention to creating as auspicious feng shui for it as we can.

It is a good idea to use a bedroom which faces in the direction which suits your personal element:

- **Fire**: south or south east

- **Water**: north

- **Wood**: east or north east

- **Metal**: west or north west

- **Earth**: south west

Check in which area of the pa kwa with enrichments your bedroom falls. If you can't manage to get your bedroom into the right enrichment or facing the right way, there is something you should be able to manage.

Lay the pa kwa over a plan of your bedroom only, with the fame enrichment over the direction the room faces, and see which part of the room to put the bed in – either a suitable enrichment within the room, or in the direction which suits your own element.

If you're not sure which way the room faces, use your intuition. Most rooms face the dominant feature such as the window, but sometimes you sense that a room faces the door, especially if there are no windows, or they are very small, or if the door is particularly large.

Do your best to make sure your bedroom falls in an enrichment which is right for you – ideally social activities, relationships or health and happiness. You can bring in remedies which suit the enrichment you would like your bedroom to be in.

GOOD FENG SHUI FOR BEDROOMS

- Check the view from the bedroom window and use strategic mirror placements where possible to reflect pleasant views into the room.

- Avoid positioning the bed with its foot facing the door: the Chinese say that this is the way dead people are laid out prior to being removed from the house – they are always carried out 'feet first'. However, you do want to be able to see who is coming in so position the bed in the corner of an octagonal arrangement if possible.

- Avoid having mirrors facing the bed

THE KITCHEN

As one of the main focal points of any house, the kitchen is the room that can benefit most from good feng shui. Because in the West kitchen units, sinks and cookers are conventionally placed against the walls of the room, it is inevitable that carrying out some tasks will cause you to have your back to people coming into the kitchen, which is not desirable. To counter this, incorporate as many mirrors as is necessary to allow you to see anyone entering or sitting behind you as you

'Island' hobs and ovens are excellent for avoiding turning your back on the main entrance while cooking. Otherwise, use mirrors (shown in blue) to allow you to see areas behind you. An alternative would be clusters of reflective appliances such as stainless steel kettles or toasters (shown in yellow).

work. Mirrors, as well as correcting the feng shui, also give the illusion of greater space and increase the light available.

The kitchen is a very yang area, and eating in here is not necessarily very relaxing. However, if what you want is stimulating conversation over meals, this may not matter to you. You can also relax better in the kitchen if it is in social activities enrichment. If you do like to entertain in the kitchen, create a more yin feel to it by lowering the lighting once the food is served: either use a dimmer switch, or turn off the main light and use only table lights.

DOORS

Doors should open opposite each other and not be off-set. If they are, use a mirror remedy as in office feng shui (*see p.118*). Position furniture as far away from inwardly opening doors as possible.Doors should open and close easily, so keep the hinges well oiled to allow easy access. If a door sticks or is badly fitting then the flow of ch'i will be disturbed. Make sure that doors are in proportion to their room size. If they are too large, they allow the ch'i to escape too rapidly but if they are too small then they restrict its access. You need to slow down or encourage the ch'i respectively so use suitable remedies to each requirement (*see pp. 98–99*).

WINDOWS

Ideally, windows should open outwards. Arched windows and octagonal windows are good feng shui. Windows with sashes that slide up and down are not helpful as they can never be opened entirely. Unless you change them (which may not be practical) you need to encourage the ch'i to enter and leave smoothly; there-fore, weather-permitting, open the top half and place plant arrangements in the bottom half.

If windows open inwards, establish the kind of ch'i

they are letting in. Opening inwards to the west could prove a problem so take remedial action by blocking excess sha ch'i either with an outward-facing mirror, a plant on the windowsill or a hanging wind-chime. Roller blinds can also be useful in countering any potentially negative effects of sha ch'i entering by the windows.

Feng Shui and the Workplace

The rules governing feng shui at work are no different to those you use at home. First draw up a ground plan of your office, shop, or factory. Overlay the pa kwa and check where everything falls. This can be an illuminating process. You may find your employees rest area in your money enrichment, or your cash register in your social enrichment.

The relationship enrichment would be your business contacts and partnerships; children would be any new projects or contracts; friends, ideally, would be your employees; and health should be your rest area. Fame and wealth are still the same.

If you work at home then you'll need to check where you've put your work area – ideally in your wealth enrichment and not in your social activities enrichment, not unless you really enjoy working. A successful TV presenter might rehearse best in their fame enrichment.

ENTRANCES AND BUILDINGS

The ideal location for your office or shop is on a corner with the entrance to your reception area cutting diagonally across the corner. This not only gives you more space for the entrance but also allows all that ch'i to funnel customers in.

You should be wary of any stairs or escalators directly facing your main entrance or all that ch'i will escape and take both your money and your customers with it.

Watch what buildings you have around you. Tall buildings to the west will provoke the unpredictable tiger ch'i and cause your business to fail unless you remedy it with concave mirrors to make the buildings appear smaller. Tall buildings to the north are protective and good.

Corner entrances are auspicious for office buildings

Make sure your reception area is spacious and welcoming. A few plants (with rounded leaves to represent money) are good to encourage customers.

Other failed businesses warn of poor feng shui for any prospective enterprise considering a move into the area

If you are looking for a new site for an office or shop you should tour the immediate area and make sure that the general area is prosperous and healthy – any closed businesses or derelict buildings are bad feng shui and you should avoid the area. Look at the road immediately outside your building. Is it like a good feng shui river – gently curving towards you bringing luck, fortune, ch'i and customers? Or is it arrowed at you, representing killing ch'i? Any roads pointed directly at your business are not good as they accelerate the ch'i too forcefully. Any business in a dead-end or cul-de-sac will suffer from stagnating ch'i and could well fail to flourish. An ideal site is where two or three roads intersect and you

have the corner position with any fast ch'i running
down the side of you rather than at you.

Keep the cash register and any financial transactions in
your wealth enrichment. You can use lots of red colour
here to encourage and attract the good fortune of the
red phoenix.

SHAPES AND SPACE

If you have your own office within a building it makes
sense to overlay the Pa kua onto a plan of it and make
sure that each enrichment is correct for maximising

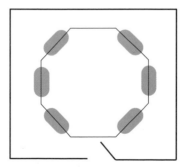

*If several people share an office the desks should be
arranged so that they form an octagon (or part of one)
rather than having the desks in straight lines*

your business. Your desk should be in the south/south-east section as this is where you will make your money and reputation.

We have to spend a lot of time in our office space so it should be as tasteful and harmonious as possible. No one should be made to sit with their back to a fellow employee nor should we have to look at large blank walls; they should be decorated with pictures of beautiful landscapes (the Chinese use scrolls with calligraphy but you may just want a watercolour).

DOORS AND WINDOWS

Doors and windows should open outwards to allow the ch'i free access. If they open inwards, you can put a small mirror onto the wall they face when open.

Remedies

Mechanical devices such as computers, telephones, photocopiers and fax machines can play too important a role in offices and this can leave workers feeling drained and tetchy by the end of the day. You can try hanging wind-chimes to add sound and movement as remedies.

A small fountain would recharge the ch'i better than anything else – you can always tell your employees it's a design feature.

Colour schemes should be kept bright and clear with white a good working colour. Pale blues will produce a calm atmosphere and only use reds if you are sure you can cope with all the extra energy it will produce. Any shadowy or rarely used corners should be lit with lamps and any sharp corners rounded off with plants. Keep any 'piped' music to a minimum as it is another remedy – and you may well not need it.

DESKS AND WORK AREAS

The really important feng shui rule is never sit with your back to the door. The reasoning behind this is you will never be able to relax and concentrate if someone could come up behind you without you knowing they were there. The Chinese say that you should always have a moment to see the person coming in so you can adopt 'superior position', which means merely being ready to accept a visitor rather than being taken by surprise.

If there are two doors into your office, you should try to position your desk so that you can see both doors, rather than have one or both behind you.

You can sit with your back to a window unless it is a west facing window. If it does face this direction and you are obliged to sit that way round you should try to have a blind or curtain at that window or a mirror facing outwards.

Here are also a few general rules to observe in the office:

1 Try to have the desk facing south/south-east to attract fame and fortune.

2 Be aware of the size of your desk as well: too large and you'll feel swamped; too small and you'll feel restricted.

3 If you use a work area, such as a shop, reception or whatever, you should do the same thing with the pa kwa and arrange your personal space accordingly.

GOOD FENG SHUI FOR DESKS

- If you overlay the pa kwa onto your desk then where you sit at the front should be regarded as your fame enrichment. Keep the keyboard here (or your notepad or whatever).

- To the left is your health area so its advisable to keep your 'out' tray here and then you can relax as each project is finished.

- To the right is your wealth enrichment – keep your 'in' tray here and may it always be full.

- Immediately opposite you at the back of the desk is your relationship enrichment – this is the place for your computer screen with whom you will be having a good relationship – hopefully.

MORE FENG SHUI FOR DESKS

- Immediately to the right is your children enrichment – a good place to keep a family photograph to remind you who you are doing it all for.

- To the left is your friends enrichment – a good place for your computer where all your files (friends) are stored.

- The left hand edge of your desk is your social activities enrichment – here you can keep your coffee and cakes.

- The right hand edge is your education enrichment so this is a good place for reference books.

Feng Shui and the Garden

In an ideal world we would have our garden on all four sides of our house:

- We could have a beautiful lawn to the south to

encourage our fame with a gentle meandering river or stream to bring us good ch'i, fame and wealth.

• We would have a high mountain to the north to nurture and protect us and it would be somewhere for all the nurturing ch'i to collect and sustain us, especially in our relationships.

• There would be gentle hills to the east to encourage the wisdom of the dragon.

• And a small lake to the west to keep the tiger at bay – not too large or the power of the tiger would become immense.

However, this is the ideal and in reality most of us have to settle for a small front garden and a larger back one if we even manage to get that. Some of us have only a few humble pot plants to keep us in touch with nature. But the principles of good feng shui for the garden remain the same whether we are cultivating ten acres or a shrub in a tub:

• Curves, curves, and more curves

• Nothing too large or small – everything in proportion.

You can think of your house as the yin aspect and your garden as the yang. Yang is all to do with light and space. The front garden is a very yang area: it's open, public, expansive. It presents your face to the outside world. The back garden, on the other hand, is the private, protected area fed by the north's nurturing ch'i – a very yin kind of place.

Even if your house doesn't face south, the front garden is still a yang area and the back garden a yin area. You need to take this into account when you assess the feng shui of both gardens, and do what you can to encourage yang ch'i at the front by opening up the south aspect to let it in, and likewise encourage the nurturing ch'i of the north into your back garden to encourage its yin nature.

Front gardens are very yang places – open and expansive – whereas back gardens are very yin – private and enclosed

In the West we think a garden is finished when we can't get any more plants in it, but in China a garden is finished when you can't take anything else away. Everybody has probably heard of, or seen, Japanese Zen gardens. These tend to be peaceful and meditative, and often minimalist in design, making good use of rocks, water, bamboo and greenery to allow ch'i to circulate gently and harmoniously. These originally started in China where formal gardening has been recorded since at least the 6th century BC and they represent the perfect ideal to aim for by incorporating a little of each of the five elements into the structure of the garden; for example:

- A pond or pool for water

- A sun dial or bronze statue for metal

- Trees and shrubs for wood

- Plenty of red and orange colours for fire

- Earth for earth.

There should be a place to sit to contemplate, a place to eat, hidden areas for surprise and excitement, and

Water elements, greenery and interesting features combine to give a garden excellent feng shui

walkways to stroll through. Compost heaps, dustbins and fuel stores should all be hidden, screen them with a trellis covered in climbers if you can or grow shrubs in front of them if you can't. If your garden is overlooked by an unpleasant view such as a factory you can always use the mirror remedy out of doors; a mirror placed in the garden does wonderful things for opening up small spaces and making them look bigger.

Even if you only have a window box or a hanging basket you can make sure it is always tidy, there are no dead plants in it, and it is healthy and full of life and colour. If you have a window box you might also want to think about the shape of it: it is better to have a window box with a curved front edge than a straight one. And it should be made of a natural material – wood or terracotta are better than plastic.

So you see, even the tiniest garden of all can still help to bring you good feng shui, if you just put a little bit of thought into it. And before you know it, you could find yourself with hanging baskets and window boxes at every window in your house. Then you'll have a garden that brings you as much good fortune as anyone else's.

GARDEN SHAPE

In the west most gardens are traditionally four-sided, and the two shapes you want to try to incorporate are the octagon and the circle. Ideally, therefore, the garden shape to aim for would be square with octagonal flower beds or lawn area with a circular pond in the centre, preferably with a fountain.

GOOD FENG SHUI IN THE GARDEN

- Any garden feature, such as a pond, that is kidney-shaped or has a harsh irregular shape is considered poor feng shui. Circular ponds are preferable.

USING THE PA KWA IN THE GARDEN

You can also draw up a pa kwa for your garden and see where the enrichments fall. You can then organise the garden layout to your benefit, placing, for example, your seat in the social activities area, the swings in the children area, and so on. The first thing to do is to overlay the pa kwa onto a plan of your garden. If you have separate front and back gardens, go through this exercise twice, once for each. If your front and back gardens join up round the side, use your judgement as to whether you have one garden or two. If they are joined by a narrow alleyway, you should probably treat them as two separate gardens. If they feel like one garden, treat them as such.

You'll have to decide for yourself whether to treat your garden as one or more sections if it's an unusual shape.

You can also consider which you would like it to be. If you have gardens on two sides of your house and you have chosen to divide them with a hedge or wall, you will probably regard them as two gardens for feng shui purposes. But if you choose to use them as a single open area, you should probably treat them as one.

Any garden that is on more than one side of the house, and is treated as one garden, is bound to have an area missing when you overlay the pa kwa onto it because the house will be occupying at least one of the enrichments. This will affect the way you use the garden and what you can get out of it. For example, if the house occupies the social activities enrichment, you may find that you can't really relax and enjoy yourself in the garden – you're always mowing lawns or weeding or creosoting the fence. If your wealth enrichment is blocked, perhaps you never have enough money to make the changes you would like in the garden. Of course, this applies to gardens that have enrichment areas missing for any reason, not just because the house is in the way.

WHICH WAY DOES THE GARDEN FACE?

In order to work out where the enrichments fall in your garden, you need to work out which way it faces. This depends on where the most commonly used entrance to it is. The front garden is the yang area – the public aspect of your garden – so it is reckoned to face in whichever direction people enter it from the outside world, usually from an outside path or driveway.

The back garden, being a yin area, belongs to the house, so it faces towards the entrance that you use yourself, which is most commonly the back door. But some gardens are not directly attached to the house, in which case the doorway or gate you enter it through is in the direction it faces. If you have a garden that leads off another one, and which you feel should be treated as a separate garden for feng shui purposes, again this is reckoned to face the entrance that you most often reach it through.

REMEDIES IN THE GARDEN

We've already looked at the eight remedies and how you use them in the house. The principles are exactly the same in the garden, but the actual remedies you use may be different. Electric lights are less often an option in the garden, for example, and it isn't recommended that you keep your television out there. So let's go through the eight remedies again, and have a look at the different ways you could use them in your garden.

1 **Light**: You may be able to light up dark areas by using garden lights, but there are plenty of other options. The simplest is to prune or cut back plants to let more light into the area, but you could also use mirrors or a pond sited in such a way that it

reflects light into the dark area. Or replant the area using plants with lighter coloured or less dense foliage.

- Use **light** as a remedy in the south and in your fame enrichment

2 **Sound**: Wind chimes are an obvious solution where you need a sound remedy, or you could use running water.

As far as the Chinese are concerned, water is an essential element in even the smallest garden. Ch'i loves water – it encourages it to flow more smoothly; remember that feng shui means 'wind and water'. A stream or fountain, or a simple feature with water trickling over stones, will create beautiful sound remedies.

Running water is the perfect sound remedy for the garden

- Use **sound** as a remedy in the north west and in your friends enrichment

3 **Colour**: This is easy in a garden when the flowers are out, but it takes more careful planning to make sure that the colour remains all year. If you have difficulty achieving this with plants, try using coloured pots, ornaments or garden seats. Red is a particularly popular colour with the Chinese because it is vibrant and stimulates ch'i to flow. But if you only need a mild effect you can use milder shades.

- Use **colour** as a remedy in the north east and in your children enrichment

4 **Life**: Something alive can encourage ch'i into corners and crannies that it otherwise misses out. Obviously, the plants in your garden are alive and so you could use them. But if you prefer you can

have a pond full of fish, which the Chinese would consider especially lucky. Or you can put a bird table in a dead space and watch the birds come to liven it up.

- Use **life** as a remedy in the south east and in your wealth enrichment

5 **Movement**: There are plenty of ways of bringing movement to a part of the garden that needs it. This is another opportunity for a bird table or moving water of some kind, such as a fountain. Or you can use wind chimes here. You could even plant something delicate that moves in the slightest breeze such as an aspen tree, or an ornamental grass with delicate fronds.

- Use **movement** as a remedy in the north and in your relationship enrichment

6 **Stillness**: If you need to slow down ch'i, try using a statue or a large urn. Some garden pots look beautiful if you leave them empty; if you choose to plant up a pot you are using as a stillness remedy, use a single plant that has a solid, simple shape, such as a clipped box tree or a yucca.

- Use **stillness** as a remedy in the west and in your pleasure enrichment.

7 **Mechanical**: Any functional object that you use in the garden can help to stir up sluggish ch'i. Perhaps this is the place to keep the barbecue? You could also put a sundial here, or the childrens' garden swing.

- Use **mechanical devices** as a remedy in the east and in your wisdom enrichment.

8 **Straight lines**: These can be either horizontal or vertical. Horizontal straight lines can be created with paths, or the edges of flower beds, or the beams across the top of a pergola. You can use arches to create vertical straight lines, or even bean-poles in the vegetable garden, or you can plant any plants with straight stems such as a standard rose.

- Use **straight lines** as a remedy in the south west and in your health enrichment.

BACKYARD GARDENING

If you haven't got a garden but just a small backyard you can still create an interesting and visually stimulating courtyard that will help the overall feng shui of your home.

Courtyards are traditional in China but they are usually in a central position with the house built around them on all four sides. Chances are yours is just a yard at the back of the house which is fine providing you don't neglect it and just use it as a place to store the dustbins. You could always use gravel over any concrete you may have and then you can change the shape to represent rivers, the sea-edge, or even waves.

You can plant climbers in tubs to cover bare brick work. You could also create an 'arbour' with a seat and a simple archway with plants growing up and over it – even try a camomile or thyme seat and enjoy that heady smell.

A clever idea I once saw was long wooden ladders attached to the walls of a courtyard with lots of pots of plants which all trailed down – it made a wonderful and interesting way of gardening in a limited space.

You could try planting wooden tubs with herbs which would be both good feng shui and useful in the kitchen.

The main thing to remember with a courtyard or backyard is not to neglect it. It should at least be swept regularly and kept tidy. And what enrichment does it fall in? This could be a valuable clue as to any problems in your life.

Wall-mounted fountains are ideal for courtyards and smaller gardens

You could even incorporate a small fountain spouting in a gentle curve from a wall into a pool where it could be re-circulated. It would take up little space but would bring movement, sound and life into an otherwise dead area.

Check what your gates into a courtyard are made of – if they are metal and in the west try to replace them with wooden ones or the tiger ch'i will be too strong.

Courtyards are invariably square-shaped so try breaking up the corners with pots, climbers or statues.

FRONT GARDEN PATHS

The path to the front of your house is considered very important – it tells the world all about you. Ideally, it should curve gently bringing your guests to you in harmony and health. Too straight or direct a path or drive will channel your guests too quickly and they will feel ill at ease.

If the path meanders too much your guests will arrive tired and bored. Entrances and paths benefit from having arches positioned along them, preferably covered with climbers. However, beware of using thorny roses as their thorns are considered poor feng shui and liable to harm your guests.

The shape of your entrance is important – what does it look like? If it widens too much ch'i will leak away. If it narrows too much ch'i will be trapped. Too harsh or angular and the ch'i will be disruptive.

> • A horseshoe-shaped drive or entrance is good as it allows the ch'i to arrive gently and be channelled away when depleted

TREES

Trees in the garden are considered essential to good feng shui but there are some principles to take note of, which are listed overleaf.

FENG SHUI FOR TREES

- Don't have trees that need radical pruning – anything that needs lopping off at the top will bring misfortune.

- Never plant a tree directly in front of your front door, it will block the arriving ch'i.

- If you don't live in a mountainous region, it's best to avoid pines and conifers.

- Ideal trees are willows, maples, apples and magnolias.

- Be wary of trees that are going to grow too big and over-shadow your house, especially any trees planted to the west of your house – tigers just love to sit and wait to pounce in them!

- Try to avoid changing the natural shape of a tree – willows and such like should be left to spread naturally.

Old age is always venerated by the Chinese, so show respect for any mature trees in your garden – even if they are tall and sharp-leaved – since their experience and accumulated wisdom can only bring good to you. Old trees, especially if they are gnarled, should never be removed: such trees have very powerful ch'i of their own and you shouldn't interfere with it.

PLANTS

Anything living creates good feng shui in the garden, and that includes plants as well as animals.

SHAPE

The important thing to consider with any kind of plant, from the tallest tree to the smallest flower, is its shape. First of all, think about the overall shape: is it tall and straight like a conifer or a bamboo, or is it rounded and curvy like a maple or a peony? In general, you should use the more rounded shapes, unless you need straight lines to move the ch'i along faster.

Curved plant shapes, rather than long, narrow forms, are generally preferred to control the flow of ch'i

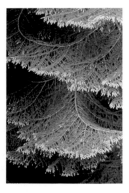

The next thing to consider is the shape of the leaves. Again, go for more rounded shapes like apple trees or nasturtiums, rather than thin, pointed leaves like pine needles or chives, unless there is a reason to go for these sharper shapes. You should also avoid plants with thorns unless they have a good scent, or a very rounded shape or leaves to counteract the sharpness of the thorns.

SCENTED PLANTS

There are certain things that will always bring good feng shui with them. One of them is sweet scents, so you can include any plant that smells beautiful regardless of its shape. Good examples of this include roses, lilies and lavender.

CLIMBERS

Climbers are very good feng shui as they allow ch'i to fall and re-circulate in the garden as well as being pleasant visual aspects. They are also excellent for hiding dustbins, and the like, as well as providing hidden areas so the whole garden can't be seen in a single glance.

Climbers along fences and walls can include roses as they are considered good for keeping out intruders (the thorns can be useful here).

PLANTS TO PROMOTE GOOD FENG SHUI

- **Trees**: oak, maples, magnolias (rounded shapes); hawthorns, horse chestnuts (rounded leaves)

- **Shrubs**: Mexican orange blossom, philadelphus, sage (rounded shapes)

- **Evergreen shrubs**: bay, laurel, box, privet (useful to provide colour all year round even if plant- or leaf-shape isn't auspicious)

- **Climbers**: clematis, honeysuckle (rounded leaves); wisteria, jasmine (scented); roses but only when strongly scented; ivy (evergreen)

- **Border plants**: anemones, poppies, daisies, peonies (rounded shape or leaves); foxgloves, irises; penstemons, lupins, hollyhocks, delphiniums (tall, spikey plants useful for stimulating stagnating or sleepy ch'i); lilies, pinks, sweet-peas, night-scented stock (scented); hellebores, bergenias, winter-flowering heather, snowdrops, primroses, spring bulbs (for year-round colour)

FLOWER BEDS

Flower beds and borders should follow much the same principle as paths: where you want to encourage the ch'i, or where you need a straight line remedy in the south west or in your health enrichment, use beds with straight edges. But where you want to calm down the flow of ch'i, use curving edges.

If you have a border with a straight back to it such as a wall or hedge, you can create flowing curves along the front edge. These should be broad, sweeping curves that don't need to be regular in shape. But island flower beds set into a lawn or into an area of paving or gravel should be a regular shape. If you need straight lines use a square or rectangular shape; if you need curves use a circular- or oval-shaped flower bed. If you are adding a flower bed to an area where the feng shui

is already nicely in balance and you don't want to upset the harmony of it, use either a circular bed or an octagonal one.

WATER FEATURES

There isn't a garden in the world that wouldn't benefit from having a pond or pool in it – even a shallow protected one if you have children. Moving water in the garden is excellent feng shui. Water encourages wildlife and brings a garden to life; it also refreshes the ch'i and soothes the nerves.

Pond edges should be raised so you can easily sit by them. Put one with goldfish in it in your money enrichment to encourage wealth. If you do have a pond make sure it is kept very clean and never allowed to stagnate or collect leaves in the autumn – this can both harm the aquatic life and cause your own ch'i to stagnate.

Garden centres sell a vast range of pond 'furniture' but only use natural materials – stone, bamboo, wood, – anything plastic is considered poor feng shui. This also applies to the construction of the pond itself. Use natural materials such as stone or wood for any visible parts of the feature. Ch'i doesn't care for impervious, man-made substances such as plastic or fibreglass.

Pools that empty into each other are considered very good as they allow ch'i to both circulate and accumulate.

Used imaginatively, garden pools can act as a wide range of remedies to suit the particular needs of your garden

WATER FEATURES AND CHILDREN

If you have young children, there are still water features that are safe to use. You can have a little water bubbling up through an arrangement of cobbles, or a fountain spilling from a wall onto paving below and flowing down through the cracks so there is no standing water anywhere. Electric pumps and other equipment for creating water features are inexpensive to buy in garden centres and are usually very straight-forward to install.

WATER AS A REMEDY

Water is the one feature that can be adapted to provide any one of the eight remedies. It can be used as a light remedy, if the surface of it reflects the light into dark areas that need lifting. It is also a sound remedy if the water can be heard moving, for example if you have a fountain. A fountainhead, a ceramic bird bath or a pool

with a mosaic bottom to it are all examples of how your water feature can bring colour to your garden. If you need a life remedy, put goldfish in the pool – this is also a movement remedy, as is a fountain or stream. A cool still pool, however small, brings stillness, and if you need a straight line remedy, create a straight sided channel to bring the water from its source into a pond. And if you need a mechanical device, what could be better than a fountain?

GARDEN FURNITURE

SEATING

You need to consider which of the enrichments you want to put a seat in. It would be ideal in your social activities area, but a seat in your fame area? Do you really want to sit back and rest on your laurels? A seat in your relationship area would be excellent if your relationship needs time for relaxation and nurturing. But some relationships need positive action to preserve them, for example, if you spend long periods apart and both have to work hard to keep the relationship flourishing. If this is the case, it may not be a good idea to sit back for too long. So think about which enrichment you want to put your garden seat in.

Having said that, it is certainly a good idea for every garden to have somewhere in it where you can sit and relax – just make sure you pick the right spot.

When it comes to choosing the seat itself, think about the shape of it, and any pattern that it incorporates. A bench seat with a slatted seat and back is made up of straight lines that will encourage ch'i. However, a wrought iron chair with a round seat and round back decorated with a pattern made up of curving flower shapes will help to slow down ch'i that is travelling too fast.

STATUES AND ORNAMENTS

Statues and ornaments are extremely useful in a garden where you need to introduce a remedy. Any coloured object can be used where a colour remedy is required, especially in the north east and in the children enrichment, for example, a coloured ceramic bird bath so the children can watch and learn about birds.

Statues are also especially useful where you need a stillness remedy. Stillness remedies are best in the west or in your social enrichment – where better to place something beautiful to look at? You can also use some statues and ornaments where you need a straight line remedy (south west, or in your health enrichment). Some abstract pieces of modern sculpture are particularly suitable for this.

ROCKERIES

A rockery should reflect the ideal layout of a home –
steep mountains to the north, gentle hills to the east,
water to the west, open areas to the south. So if you
have a pond in your garden, hopefully in the west, the
rockery should go to the east. Rockeries should be
planned deliberately and not be used to camouflage
piles of left-over stones and they should look as natural
as possible. You can always incorporate wood (as one
of the elements) into your rockery in the form of drift
wood or ancient branches.

ADVANCED FENG SHUI

Now that we have explored the principles underlying
feng shui and seen how these are applied to various
aspects of our surroundings, in this chapter we will
look more closely at more advanced elements of feng
shui, some of which have been mentioned briefly in
previous chapters.

The Lo P'an Geomancy Compass

As we've seen, the traditional feng shui compass, the lo
p'an, is used to determine the orientation of internal
and external locations, to assess the flow of ch'i
through them and so determine the suitability of the
location for its owner or purpose. It is used most often
when a site is being assessed before being built on or to
determine the best orientations for graves.

Compasses tend to vary in design depending on the
manufacturer, but all possess common elements. The lo
p'an is circular (symbolising heaven) and set into a
square base (symbolising the earth), around which it
can be rotated. In its centre is a conventional compass,
the needle of which gives emphasis to the south.
Radiating out from the centre is a circular grid made up

of a number of rings, each division of which contains a
Chinese character.

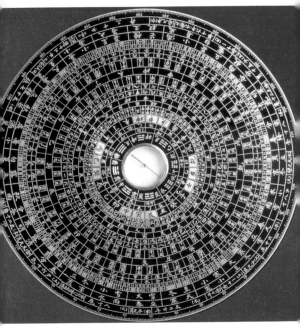

The dial of a lo p'an showing the complex make-up of the rings

The number of rings on the dial varies depending on the size of the lo p'an but invariably there are three rings of essential information. The following is a list of what is on these rings from an 'average' compass.

THE HEAVEN PLATE

- Trigrams of Former Heaven Sequence
- Symbols of the 9 stars
- The 24 mountains
- The 8 major planets
- The 64 hexagrams
- The 64 hexagrams changing
- The 24 fortnights of the year
- The 28 auspicious burial constellations
- The 360 degrees of the compass
- The 72 dragon's veins of ch'i
- Mountains and the dragon's veins

THE HUMAN PLATE

- Stems and branches of a person's horoscope
- The 60 points of good and bad luck

- The spirit paths of the dead
- Earth and mountain hexagrams for auspicious sites to live
- Auspicious sites for burial
- Division into the five aspects and the horoscope
- Yin and yang
- Auspicious river directions
- Auspicious burial near rivers
- The dead and ch'i
- Good and bad positions for burial
- Further burial advice
- The five aspects and the dead
- The Nine Palaces
- The ruling planet of the deceased
- The 24 mountains
- The Three Guardian Spirits
- The 12 Gods
- The 31 auspicious points of the soul
- The horoscope of the deceased

THE EARTH PLATE

- The five aspects of the deceased
- The 60 Dragon Points
- Actual reference point of the site
- The Two Branches of the Dead
- The 28 Constellations

As can be gathered from even a scant description such as this, interpreting the lo p'an is not for the beginner and can only seriously be undertaken by masters with considerable knowledge of both Chinese astrology and geomancy.

The Geomancy Ruler

Another tool used by the more experienced feng shui practitioner is the geomancy ruler. This is used primarily to measure the various dimensions of a room or its contents since the Chinese believe both the size and proportion of such items as rooms, doors and furniture, can have a direct bearing on the good fortune (or otherwise) of the owner or occupier. For example, a desk that was between 58–60 cm long, 33–34 cm wide and 32–33 cm high would be considered well proportioned and very auspicious indeed.

The ruler itself looks much like an ordinary steel

retractable ruler does except that it has a few extra measurements. The two outside edges have conventional measurements in metres and feet and inches while the two inner strips contain information which relates to the eight enrichments (*see p.30*). One strip gives the measurements for internal readings while the other gives the measurements for outdoor readings.

Commonly, the information on the geomancy ruler is marked in red and black characters: those in black indicate auspicious measurements while those in red are inauspicious. Examples of 'good' and 'bad' dimensions and their indications are shown below.

GOOD AND BAD DIMENSIONS

Length (cm)	Portent	Indication
0 – 5.4	Good	Fortune
5.5 – 10.7	Bad	Sickness
10.8 – 16.1	Bad	Divorce
16.2 – 21.4	Good	Fairness
21.5 – 26.8	Good	Promotion
26.9 – 32.1	Bad	Theft
32.2 – 37.5	Bad	Accident
37.6 – 42.9	Good	Origin

See pages 181–184 for a list of possible suppliers of such rulers.

Numbers

A feng shui practitioner would use the ruler and compass to accurately measure your home and assess its suitability for you, but to continue their consultation they would also need some information from you to work out your *kua* numbers: your lucky and unlucky numbers. These are important because using them you can work out which are your most auspicious directions, in other words, the directions you should face while doing a variety of fundamental actions, such as eating, studying or even sleeping.

Kua numbers are determined by the year of your birth and your sex.

FEMALE LUCKY AND UNLUCKY NUMBERS

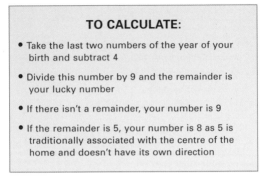

TO CALCULATE:

- Take the last two numbers of the year of your birth and subtract 4

- Divide this number by 9 and the remainder is your lucky number

- If there isn't a remainder, your number is 9

- If the remainder is 5, your number is 8 as 5 is traditionally associated with the centre of the home and doesn't have its own direction

For example, if you were born in 1961,

- The last two digits of your birth year are 61

- Subtract 4 to give 58

- Divide this by 9 which gives a remainder of 4 (since 9 x 6 = 54).

Thus, 4 is your lucky number.

MALE LUCKY AND UNLUCKY NUMBERS

TO CALCULATE:

- Take the last two numbers of your birth and subtract them from 100

- Divide this number by 9 and the remainder is your lucky number

- If there isn't a remainder, your number is 9

- If the remainder is 5, your lucky number is 2 as 5 is traditionally associated with the centre of the home and doesn't have its own direction

For example, if you were born in 1950,

- The last two digits of your birth year are 50

- Subtract this number from 100 to give 50

- Divide this by 9 which gives a remainder of 5 (since 9 x 5 = 45).

Therefore, your lucky number becomes 2.

HOW TO USE YOUR LUCKY NUMBERS

To find our most auspicious directions, we need to refer back to the lo shu magic square (see p.24) with the directions on it:

4 Early Summer South East	9 Fire Summer South	2 Late Summer South West
3 Wood Spring East	5 Earth	7 Metal Autumn West
8 Late Winter North East	1 Water Winter North	6 Early Winter North West

From your lucky number you can now see your lucky direction; for example, if your lucky number is 6 then your lucky direction is south east and your lucky 'season' is early summer. The following table examines these numbers and directions in a little more detail. The unlucky direction listed is a bad place for your house to face and would need remedying.

AUSPICIOUS AND INAUSPICIOUS

No.	Lucky Direction	Season	Unlucky Direction
1	North	Winter	South East
2	South West	Later Summer	North West
3	East	Spring	West
4	South East	Early Summer	North
6	North West	Early Winter	South West
7	West	Autumn	East
8	North East	Late Winter	South
9	South	Summer	North East

Colours

Each of these eight 'lucky' directions and numbers also has a 'lucky' colour traditionally associated with it.

These colours should be chosen for clothes if you want to lift your spirit or change your luck. They can also be incorporated into decor and furnishings.

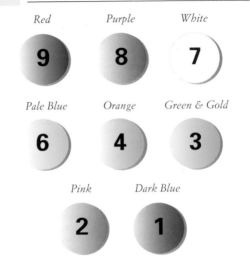

Lucky colour and number associations

Chinese Astrology

We saw earlier how each of the Chinese astrological animal signs has a 'lucky' or natural direction (*see p.00*). However, each animal sign has a whole variety of such associations, linking it to times of the year and even times of each day which are auspicious. (If you don't already know which animal sign you were born under, you can find this out from the chart on pages 43–48).

TIMES OF THE YEAR

Each animal sign is associated with certain periods of the year which are roughly equivalent to the Western zodiac. This may explain why you may feel 'better' or happier at certain times of the year. The following table outlines how the signs and periods match up.

Chinese Sign	Auspicious time of year	Western Equivalent
Rat	mid Nov. – mid Dec.	Sagittarius
Ox	mid Dec. – mid Jan.	Capricorn
Tiger	mid Jan. – mid Feb.	Aquarius
Hare	mid Feb. – mid Mar.	Pisces
Dragon	mid Mar. – mid Apr.	Aries
Snake	mid Apr. – mid May	Taurus
Horse	mid May – mid Jun.	Gemini
Goat	mid Jun. – mid Jul	Cancer
Monkey	mid Jul. – mid Aug.	Leo
Cockerel	mid Aug. – mid Sept.	Virgo
Dog	mid Sep. – mid Oct	Libra
Pig	mid Oct. – mid Nov.	Scorpio

TIMES OF DAY

The following table shows the times of day when people born under each animal sign will function best. They are said to be the times of day when you should make decisions. Put off anything important until 'your' time of day is reached and then you will feel better able to cope.

Chinese Sign	Auspicious time of day
Rat	11 pm – 1 am
Ox	1 am – 3 am
Tiger	3 am – 5 am
Hare	5 am – 7 am
Dragon	7 am – 9 am
Snake	9 am – 11 am
Horse	11 am – 1 pm
Goat	1 pm – 3 pm
Monkey	3 pm – 5 pm
Cockerel	5 pm – 7 pm
Dog	7 pm – 9 pm
Pig	9 pm – 11 pm

ANIMALS' COMPATIBILITY

Each of the animals also has a 'compatibility' with other animals, which may explain why there is empathy or tension in a household with more than one person sharing.

In the diagram below, each of the animals is said to have two close allies and one deadly foe. The allies can be easily identified by seeing which two animals make up the three points of a triangle with you. And the deadly adversary is, of course, the animal directly opposite you.

Elements

Each of the lucky numbers and directions also has a 'lucky' element traditionally associated with it. These are:

- 1 : greater fire
- 2 : lesser wood
- 3 : greater metal
- 4 : lesser water
- 6 : lesser fire
- 7 : greater wood
- 8 : lesser metal
- 9 : greater water

A *greater element* is represented as a much stronger form of it while a *lesser element* is represented as a softer version. For example, a combine harvester might be a greater metal but an axe would be lesser; a raging inferno of a forest fire would be greater fire whilst a candle flame would be a lesser fire; an ocean might be greater water but a mountain stream a lesser one; a huge forest a greater wood whilst a single branch a lesser one.

Once you know your number (*see pp.154–155*) you can find your element from the list above. Each has its opposite and tension in a house can be caused by opposites trying to live together without compromise or acceptance of the other's position. You would need a greater rather than lesser water to quench a greater fire and likewise a lesser metal would be pretty useless against a greater wood. However. all things can be accomplished given time and lateral thinking. You might believe a lesser metal axe trying to live with a greater wood forest would have little chance of success but over time even a tiny axe could fell an entire forest, piece by piece.

The inter-relationship of the elements is shown below.

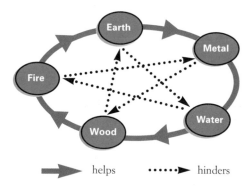

Earth

Metal

Fire

Water

Wood

——▶ helps   •••••▶ hinders

Elements that are next to each other in the cycle help each other; thus, water helps wood, wood helps fire, and so on. On the other hand, elements that are opposite each other hinder each other in the sequence shown by the dotted lines on the diagram; so, water hinders fire, fire hinders metal, etc. This holds true for lesser or greater elements equally.

PHYSICAL QUALITIES OF THE ELEMENTS

The elements also have their physical manifestations as well as their psychological. For instance, if you are a greater metal type you may find that living in an all-wood house would be unsettling. Likewise, a water type living inland and far from any water would find it very difficult, while a wood type living in a modern metal construction could find it uncomfortable and disquieting. You need to choose your home according to your element type:

- **Metal** – modern constructions that use a lot of steel.

- **Water** – near rivers or the sea.

- **Wood** – houses built mainly out of wood or near forests and woods.

- **Fire** – hot places, noisy, crowded 'combustible' places.

- **Earth** – central places, basements, mid terraces, brick or stone houses.

HOUSE STYLES AND THE ELEMENTS

Each of the five element types is most comfortable in a different type of house.

FIRE

- **Style:** A north-facing, comfortable, warm house but quite grand, like a manor house.

- **Good interior colours:** reds, oranges.

- **Key word:** passion.

The ideal Fire house

WATER

- **Style:** a south-facing, older, more traditional house, like a period thatched cottage.

- **Good interior colours:** black, dark blues.

- **Key word:** imagination.

WOOD

- **Style:** a west-facing, unusual, distinctive or individual house such as a lighthouse or castle.

- **Good interior colours:** green, gold.

- **Key word:** competitive.

METAL

- **Style:** an east-facing, modern, designer house.

- **Good interior colours:** white, grey, pale blues.

- **Key word:** order.

EARTH

- **Style:** a mid-terrace would be perfect or a basement flat but it would have to be family-oriented.

- **Good interior colours:** yellow, pale green and brown, dark grey.

- **Key word:** nurturing.

CHOOSING YOUR IDEAL HOUSE

When trying to work out your ideal home, it is best to use both your birth year element and your animal element. For example, if you were born in 1958 this would make you earth (from the year; *see p.46*) and fire (from the animal, which in this case is a dog; *see p.46 & 51*). Thus, in seeking your ideal home you would try to find one which was a combination of the ideal types of both elements: your ideal home would thus be a grand (fire) family-oriented (earth) one. Another example of how to tie the two types of elements together would be where someone is metal (from their year) and water (from their animal). Ideally they may go for a period home (water) but it would need to be ordered and neat (metal).

+

=

Combining your elements to identify your ideal house style

ELEMENTS WITHIN THE HOME

You should also try to make use of your elements within the home. For example, if your lucky number is 6 which would give you a lucky direction of north west (*see p.157*) and a lucky element of lesser fire (*see below*) you could try placing candles in the north west corner of your home to balance the energy and keep everything healthy. Likewise, put candles in your 'unlucky' direction (which in the case of 6 would be south west) to minimise the negative influences coming from this direction.

LUCKY REMEDIES FOR THE HOME

- 1 (greater fire) – an open fire
- 2 (lesser wood) – a piece of drift wood
- 3 (greater metal) – a large metal statue
- 4 (lesser water) – dish of water, vase of flowers with water
- 6 (lesser fire) – candles, night-lights
- 7 (greater wood) – a tree or large indoor plant
- 8 (lesser metal) – three metal coins
- 9 (greater water) – a fountain

You can play around with these elements and their remedies and come up with your own. To be most effective, you should place one in the lucky direction and a balancing one in the unlucky direction.

Improving Ch'i

Irrespective of how much detail you want to go into with your feng shui, there are various simple rules to follow to improve your home. You may not want to get involved with compass directions, elements, astrology or yin and yang but you might feel that an understanding of how ch'i energy operates could be beneficial, as indeed it can.

Ch'i flows as and when it wants but it does have certain 'preferences' and there is a lot you can do to help its flow and in doing so, help yourself.

The following panels will give you some idea of the 'good' flow of ch'i; what it likes and dislikes; how it can be enhanced; and how to stop it degenerating into unhelpful or even positively harmful *sha*.

All of these may give you an idea of how and why ch'i moves as it does and remember that movement is what ch'i is all about. There is a constant movement from yin to yang and from yang to yin. There is nothing you can do about this: ch'i cannot be stopped, merely aided or hindered.

CH'I LIKES

- brightness, harmony, order, curves, cleanliness, tidiness, order, tranquillity, peace and 'good taste'

- freedom to wander at will and not to be 'directed' too strongly

- being welcomed and guided rather than having order imposed on it by force

- having its seasons and rhythms understood and accepted rather than being expected to adhere to our concept of the world

- to be useful and to bring positive good health and 'luck' rather than being ignored and unused.

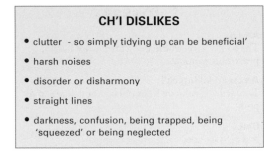

CH'I DISLIKES

- clutter - so simply tidying up can be beneficial'

- harsh noises

- disorder or disharmony

- straight lines

- darkness, confusion, being trapped, being 'squeezed' or being neglected

Hopefully, what you have learned in this book will help you begin to be able to maximise the flow of ch'i through your surroundings and with the consequent improvement in your life and fortunes.

Glossary

An Lu
The south west, whose enrichments are health, peace and happiness

Arrowed killing ch'i
Two or more straight lines of ch'i converging to a point

Chai
A dwelling; houses

Chang Yin
The west, whose enrichments are pleasure and indulgence

Chen
The Arousing trigram whose associations are late winter; the north east; wood; thunder

Ch'i
Cosmic energy

Ch'ien
The Creative trigram whose associations are heaven; summer; south; fire

Chin
The element metal

Chin Ts'ai
The north west, whose enrichments are friends and new beginnings

Chin Yin
The north, whose enrichment is relationships

Enrichments
The eight areas of life situations, each of which is associated with one of the trigrams that can be found on the pa kwa

Fa Chan
The east, whose enrichments are wisdom and experience

Fan ch'i
Offensive ch'i; residual emotions

Fang
Inner

Feng
Wind

Feng Huang
The Red Phoenix of the south, one of the four celestial animals of Chinese mythology

Feng shui
Wind/water, the system of arranging the environ-

ment around us to maximise the flow of ch'i;
Chinese geomancy

Feng shui hsien-sheng
A feng shui consultant or practitioner

H'sun
The Wind trigram whose associations are gentle; late
summer; the south west; wood

Hsin
The heart; ourselves

Hsueh
Surroundings

Huan Lo
The south east, whose enrichment is wealth

Huo
Fire

I Ching
The Book of Changes, one of the most sacred and
ancient Chinese texts

Jen Hsin
The Centre

K'an
The Dangerous trigram whose associations are the
west; autumn; metal; the moon

Ken
The Mountain trigram whose associations are early winter; the north west; calm

Killing ch'i
Inauspicious ch'i flowing too fast in a straight line

K'un
The Receptive trigram whose associations are winter; the north; water; creation

Li
The Clinging trigram whose associations are spring; the east; wood; the sun

Liu
Trees; gardens; willows

Lo p'an
The feng shui compass

Lo Shu
The three-by-three square arrangement of the numbers 1 to 9 in such a way that adding together the sum of any three numbers in a straight line totals 15. This 'magic square' has great symbolic importance in Chinese culture

Lung mei
The paths that ch'i follows, literally 'the dragon's veins'

Mu
The element wood

Pa kwa
The octagonal diagnostic tool which uses the eight trigrams and their various associations to determine areas in which ch'i flow requires improvement

Sha
Unhealthy ch'i, literally 'noxious vapour'

Sha ch'i
Disruptive ch'i from the west

Shan
Mountains

Shan shui
Mountains and water; a style of Chinese landscape painting

Shao Yang
East or Lesser Yang

Shao Yin
West or Lesser Yin

Sheng ch'i
Wise or growing ch'i from the east

Shui
Water

T'ai Ch'i
The Supreme Ultimate

T'ai ch'i chuan
A Chinese martial art

T'ai Yang
South or Great Yang

T'ai Yin
North or Great Yin

Tao
Literally 'The Way', Taoism is a religion, a philosophy and a way of life; at its core is the Universal Principle, in which heaven and earth co-exist in perfect harmony

T'ien ch'ai
The north east whose enrichments are children and family

Trigram
A symbol composed of different combinations of three solid and broken lines; the top line of the trigram represents heaven, the middle line humankind and the bottom line earth

T'sang ch'i
Nurturing or hidden ch'i from the north

Ts'ang feng
A cold, hidden wind that blows from hollows and can cause ill health

T'u
The element earth

Tui
The Lake trigram, whose associations are early summer; the south east; metal; joy

Wang Ts'ai
The south, whose enrichments are fame and prosperity

Wen
The Gold or Green Dragon of the east, one of the four celestial animals of Chinese mythology

Wu
The White Tiger of the west, one of the four celestial animals of Chinese mythology

Wu Hsing
The five elements or aspects: wood, fire, earth, metal and water

Yang
One of the two opposite but complimentary cosmic forces which shape the universe and everything in it; yang is positive, creative energy

Yang ch'i
Invigorating or nourishing ch'i from the south

Yin
One of the two opposite but complimentary cosmic forces which shape the universe and everything in it; yin is negative, receptive energy

Yuan Wu
The Black Tortoise of the north, one of the four celestial animals of Chinese mythology

Useful Addresses

UNITED KINGDOM

Feng Shui Network International
P. O. Box 2133
London
W1A 1RL

Tel: +44-(0)7000 336474

The Feng Shui Society
40 Lammas Park Rd
London
W5 5JB

Tel: +44-(0)7050 289200

The Feng Shui Association
31 Woburn Place
Brighton
BN1 9GA

Tel/fax: +44-(0)1273 693844

The Feng Shui Company
Ballard House
37 Norway Street
Greenwich
London
SE10 9DD

Tel: +44-(0)7000 781901

The Geomancer & Feng Shui Store
PO Box 250
Woking
Surrey
GU21 1YJ

Tel: +44-(0)7000 888989

UNITED STATES

Earth Design Inc.
PO Box 530725
Miami Shores
Florida 33153

Tel: +1-305 756 6426
Fax: +1-305 751 9995

The Feng Shui Institute of America
PO Box 488
Wabasso
Florida 32970

Tel: +1-407 589 9900
Fax: +1-407 589 1611

The Feng Shui Warehouse
PO Box 3005
San Diego
California 92163

Tel: +1-619 523 2158
Fax: +1-619 523 2165

AUSTRALIA

Feng Shui Design Studio
PO Box 705
Glebe
Sydney
NSW 2037

The Feng Shui Society of Australia
PO Box 1565
Rozelle
Sydney
NSW 2039

Feng Shui and the Internet

There is a lot of information on the internet about feng shui and the following is a list of addresses that you might like to begin exploring from. Happy surfing!

http://www.lmcinet.com/amfengshui
American Feng Shui Institute's home page website.

http://www.ozemail.com.au./bmtv/fengshui.htm
Feng shui advice, videos, news letters, remedies.

http://downtown.wcb.aol.com/ads/cats/cat_ homegarden7txt.html
Home and garden feng shui including bonsai trees.

http://www.spiritweb.org/Spirit/feng-shui-liu-07.html
Feng shui and love. Promotes spiritual consciousness on the internet. Healing schools and techniques of feng shui and ch'i.

http://www.spiritweb.org/Spirit/feng-shui-liu-05.html
Feng Shui and astrology.

http://www.fsgallery.com/
Feng shui gallery of calligraphy and art. A gallery of

Chinese and Japanese art and calligraphy.

http://www.cwo.com/~ashlin/shui8.html

Feng Shui: The Chinese art of design and placement reviews. Two internationally sought-after consultants offer a history of this venerable art, and guidance on how to use it effectively.

http://www.mistral.co.uk./hammerwood/dowser.htm

Feng shui, earth acupuncture, geomancy, dowsing, geopathic stress, white and black streams, healing streams, ley lines, earth mysteries, earth healing, watercourses, underground water.

http://www.meltzerfengshui.com/

Creating heaven on earth. Carol Meltzer Feng Shui Designs. Functional art gallery.

http://www.cwo.com/~ashlin/flutes.html"

Feng Shui flutes and word stones.

http://www.asiaconnect.com.my/lillian-too/fundamental/

Fundamentals of feng shui, the trinity of luck, order and form.

http:///www.community.net/~sgxenja/index.html

Seann Xenja's home page. Welcome to the world of Feng Shui. The web site of a feng shui consultant.

http://www.intersurf.com/locale/geo/
Geomancy Dragon Feng Shui Education
Organisation.

Further Reading

FENG SHUI

An Anthropological Analysis of Chinese Geomancy
Stephen Feuchtwang, SMC, 1974

Change your Life with Feng Shui
Li Pak Tin & Helen Yeap, Quantum, 1997

Feng Shui for Beginners
Richard Craze, Hodder & Stoughton, 1996

Feng Shui For Cats
Roni Jay, Thorsons, 1998

Feng Shui in your Garden
Roni Jay, Thorsons, 1998

Feng Shui Made Easy
William Spear, Thorsons, 1995

Feng Shui
Angel Thompson, St. Martin's Griffin, 1995

Feng Shui
Kirsten M. Lagatree, Newleaf, 1996

Garden Feng Shui – A Beginner's Guide
Roni Jay, Hodder & Stoughton, 1999

Interior Design with Feng Shui
Sarah Rossbach, Rider Books, 1987

Practical Feng Shui
Richard Craze, Anness, 1997

Sacred Gardens
Roni Jay, Thorsons, 1998

Teach Yourself Feng Shui
Richard Craze and Roni Jay, Hodder & Stoughton, 1998

The Complete Illustrated Guide to Feng Shui
Lillian Too, Element Books, 1996

The Elements of Feng Shui
Man-Ho Kwok with Joanne O'Brien, Element Books, 1991

The Feng Shui Game Pack
Richard Craze, Godsfield Press and HarperCollins, 1997

The Feng Shui Kit
Man-Ho Kwok, Piatkus, 1995

The Feng Shui Pack
Richard Craze, Godsfield Press & HarperCollins, 1997

The Living Earth manual of Feng Shui, Chinese Geomancy
Stephen Skinner, Arkana, 1982

The Western Guide to Feng Shui
Terah Kathryn Collins, Hay House Inc., 1995

CHINESE PHILOSOPHY

Between Heaven and Earth
Harriet Beinfield & Efrem Korngold, Ballantine
Books, 1991

Collins Gem Chinese Astrology
Bridget Giles & The Diagram Group,
HarperCollins, 1996

Chinese Horoscopes for Beginners
Kristyna Arcarti, Hodder & Stoughton, 1995

Chinese Mythology
Derek Walters, The Aquarian Press, 1992

Lao Tzu's TAO TE CHING
Timothy Freke (ed), Piatkus, 1995

Teach Yourself Chinese Astrology
Richard Craze, Hodder & Stoughton, 1997

The Fundamental Principles of the Yi-king Tao
Veolita Parke Boyle, W & G Foyle, 1934

The I Ching and Mankind
Diana ffarington Hook, Routledge & Kegan Paul,
1975

The I Ching Workbook
R. L. Wing, Aquarian, 1983

The Secret of the Golden Flower
Richard Wilhelm, Routledge & Kegan Paul, 1974

The Way of Life
Witter Bynner, Perigee Books,1944

CHINESE HEALTH

Chi Kung
James MacRitchie, Element, 1995

Chinese Herbal Medicine
Richard Craze, Piatkus, 1996

Teach Yourself Traditional Chinese Medicine
Richard Craze, Hodder & Stoughton, 1997

The Complete Illustrated Guide to Chinese Medicine
Tom Williams, Element Books, 1997

GENERAL

Cambridge Illustrated History of China
Patricia Buckley Ebrey, Cambridge University Press,
1996

China, Land of Discovery and Invention
Robert Temple, Patrick Stephens, 1986

Imperial China
Charis Chan, Penguin Books, 1991

The Changing Society of China
Ch'u Chai & Winberg Chai, Mentor Books, 1962